46 - brands & relationships
43 - 4 steps to m.
48 - honeybees
72 - cust. value
73 - resume & LI tweak =
76 → marriott → crm
77 - cus. value #table & quote!
86 - cust. loyalty
87 - Lexus vs Infiniti
89 - Best Buy Twitter
92 - complaint discovery

MW01026385

CUSTOMER EXPERIENCE

What, How and Why Now

DON PEPPERS

ISBN: 978-1-48356-015-1

Customer Experience: What, How and Why Now

CONTENTS

CUSTOMER EXPERIENCE:
WHAT, HOW, AND WHY NOW

Foreword

In just the last 20 years, technological progress the business world over has irreversibly transformed the nature of business competition.

Because of technology, customers are far more empowered than ever before—more knowledgeable, more connected to other customers, more discerning. And customers have higher standards today. They expect more. They demand it.

Because of technology, entrepreneurs scour the ever-changing business landscape to find the next disruptive innovation, while established companies struggle to anticipate and defend against having their own business models disrupted. But today's customers have zero tolerance for a substandard experience with any product or service, so it turns out that customers themselves are the biggest disruptors of all.

The result is that literally every business on the planet seems to be engaged in some type of customer-oriented initiative or another, just trying to stay one step ahead of their customers' demands, or at least trying not to fall too far behind them.

The task that businesses are taking on goes by a number of different labels and buzzwords. Some refer to it in terms of "customer centricity." What does it take for an enterprise to differentiate itself by putting the customer at the center of its business, and then serving customers better than its competitors do? Others may refer to it as "customer engagement," or perhaps "customer relationship management," and they search for the mechanisms, strategies, and offerings most likely to entice customers into long-lasting, loyal relationships based on trust.

But what all these initiatives have in common, what every one of them takes as a first principle, is that to be successful they must see the business through the customer's own eyes. They must *experience* what the customer experiences, and then take steps to ensure that this experience becomes better, easier, more convenient, more enjoyable, more useful, and appropriate for the customer. And they do this because they hope that a customer experience that is better for a customer will be more profitable for the enterprise, as well.

The central task companies are grappling with, in other words, is managing and improving each individual customer's experience with their brand or product. They want to use technology to deliver the right experience to the right customer at the right time.

It takes effort and resources to improve the customer's experience. Yes, new technologies need to be employed, but new tasks also have to be accomplished, processes must be altered, and people must be paid. A large part of any improvement in the customer experience will come simply from eliminating all the obstacles and "friction" a customer has to deal with just to meet whatever need they're trying to meet.

In the contact center space, for instance, when a company resolves an issue on the customer's very first call, it eliminates friction in the experience. The irony is that when a company eliminates friction, it not only improves customer satisfaction and loyalty; it also reduces its own costs, because fewer calls will have to be handled, and fewer problems will have to be dealt with later.

But technology waits for no one. It doesn't slow its pace to allow us mere mortals to catch up. If we want to be competitively successful, we have to think more quickly and act more expeditiously. In fact, we have to change our companies at least at a rate that matches technology's accelerating speed, just to keep up with our customers' ever increasing expectations. This is why today's businesses all want to become more customer-oriented right away—*yesterday*, if that were at all possible.

Still, while technology may be driving this massive, worldwide transformation of business, a customer's experience, by its very nature, is based on *humanity*. Computers and automated systems may render products and services ever more efficient, but machines don't buy anything. They aren't acquisitive. They have no needs to meet, no problems to solve, no mouths to feed.

Only humans are customers. And while they do respond to the features and attributes of personalized services and products, they also crave empathy, creativity, humor, irony, and the sense of emotional fulfillment that comes from accomplishing new things or mastering new tasks. Above all, human beings want to *connect* with other human beings, to feel a part of something bigger, to belong.

Technology by itself simply cannot fulfill these human cravings, but it can still empower and augment the efforts of a company's employees to do so. Delivering humanity to customers is an essential element in providing a higher-quality customer experience, and with technology a company can deliver humanity *at scale*. But, this requires considerably more than writing a few choice lines of code or putting together a few well-integrated business process rules.

To manage individual customer experiences, a company has to have the right technological capabilities, including data systems, analytics, and interactive platforms. But it also has to ensure that its organization is properly aligned, so that it can see and manage the customer experience even as it is being influenced by the actions and reactions of multiple different business units and interactions, across the whole range of channels.

Moreover, because it will never be possible to automate everything no matter how advanced the technology becomes, and because human-to-human interaction is the only sufficient way to inject humanity into the process, the people within the organization will need to have the right mind-set—a mind-set that predisposes them to make the right decisions with respect to protecting customer interests, and to take the right actions even in the absence of plans, algorithms, or scripts.

Delivering a better customer experience represents an immense problem to solve, even for a company with no cumbersome industrial-era baggage. And with every new interactive platform or mobile app, the urgency of solving it only intensifies, as customers become even more informed, even more demanding and impatient.

This book is designed to help.

CHAPTER 1

Technology Drives the Customer Experience Movement

The customer experience business revolution is driven by information technology.

Not that providing a good customer experience hasn't always been a good thing to do anyway, because it has. But the customer experience has only become the central focus for so many businesses because of information technologies developed in the last two decades or so.

If you were a small proprietor in the 1800s, you worried about each customer's experience with your product or service, because you met with and served each customer personally. With the introduction of assembly lines and industrial processes, mass-produced products could be delivered at a fraction of the cost, but the personal touch had to be eliminated, because it was so costly.

Instead, customers became the *objects* of a company's competitive strategy. Ever lower manufacturing and transactional costs drove real benefits for consumers, but with each dollar of cost saved, the relative cost of trying to maintain an individual customer relationship became that much more significant. There simply was no practical, cost-efficient way to pay attention to thousands, or millions, of customers individually. Mass marketing came to depend on branding to reassure customers of their products' quality.

But computer technology has changed all that, allowing businesses to once again try to engage their individual customers in ongoing relationships. Customer databases, analytical tools, interactivity, and mass customization processes – all these computer-mediated capabilities now make it possible once again to pay attention to customers as individuals, and to manage each customer's individual customer experience. Even when you have millions of them.

Where Technology Meets Humanity

For the first 100,000 years or so of the human race's existence, the average human being lived on the equivalent of perhaps $400 to $600 per year in resources. Year after year, from century to century, millennium on millennium, the population grew, continents were explored, and settlements expanded, but on a per capita basis people were no better off, economically. Only a few rulers and other powerful people ever lived on much more than a few hundred dollars' worth of resources a year.

It wasn't until the Industrial Revolution in the 1700s that people *on average* began to get wealthier with time. It was only then that mothers and fathers first began expecting that their children would be able to eat more regularly and have more things than they themselves had had.

The rate of growth in per capita wealth in the industrialized world was about 0.75 percent per year in the 1700s but by 1900 it had grown to about 1.5 percent per year, and by the middle of the 20th century per capita wealth was increasing by almost 2.5 percent per year. Technological innovation is what is driving this faster and faster economic growth, and it means more than just comfort. It means that fewer people die of disease or hunger, natural disasters are easier to deal with, and life spans continue to increase.

Worldwide, the average human life span today is increasing at the rate of about five hours every single day! This means that the average baby born today can expect to live about two months longer than the average baby born one year ago.

Obviously, Malthus was wrong. Thomas Robert Malthus, the English economist, famously predicted in the 1700s that populations would grow geometrically, while resources only grew arithmetically, so sooner or later we would run out of resources entirely and we'd all starve. It turns out, however, that the more people we have, the faster technology accelerates (because there are more brains at work combining ideas), and one of the most important benefits of new technology is that the same amount of food, shelter, and comfort for any single individual can be produced with fewer resources.

But rapid technological progress has extremely important implications for businesses. Used to be you could launch a business and, if you were successful, you'd have several generations' worth of profit to harvest. This is no longer true. Launch a business these days and you'll be lucky if your whole business model hasn't been outdated or overturned by some new technology within just a decade or two.

The Iridium system, for instance, a low-earth-orbit network of satellites designed to facilitate mobile phone communication without cell towers, was technologically outdated within about 10 years of its design. The technology was to involve 77 satellites (iridium is the 77th element in the Periodic Table), but the business plan was architected in the mid-1980s, and by 1998, when 66 of the satellites had been launched and the system was deployed, the whole idea had been outdated. The company filed for Chapter 11 in 2000, costing its original investors some $5 billion.

So, the first lesson we should draw from this accelerating rush of technological progress is that for any business to be successful today, it's not enough just to have a new idea. You need to be able to produce new ideas continuously. You can't generate profit for long from any single innovation, no matter how brilliant it is. Increasingly, the only way you'll be able to sustain a business is through sustained innovation.

But the second lesson to draw from technology's rush is that the nature of business competition itself has been fundamentally altered. Information technology now permits companies to remember and interact with millions of individual customers, one customer at a time. Technology allows a business to treat different customers differently, providing each individual customer with an individually configured product or service, along with individually relevant messaging or offers.

Instead of having to focus on just a single product or service at a time and then advertising to broad populations of potential customers in order to sell as much of that product as they can, today's marketers increasingly focus on one customer at a time, and try to gain as much business from that customer as possible, over the lifetime of that customer's patronage.

Businesses today are obsessed with managing the *experience* that each individual customer has with their product, their service, their brand.

But, no matter how automated their systems are, or how flawlessly their web sites and mobile apps render these experiences, if companies want their customers to stay with them from product to product, business model to business model, they will need their trust. And trust is not technological at all. It is a deeply human quality.

People trust other people. They don't trust bureaucracies, processes, policies, or machines. They trust their family, their friends, their colleagues and compatriots. So, if a business wants its customers' trust, then it has to figure out how to use its technology to deliver its own humanity.

The customer experience itself is where technology meets humanity.

Are Your Customers Assets? Or Obstacles?

Sometimes a counter-intuitive idea can seem interesting simply because it is unorthodox. And sometimes the reason it sounds counter-intuitive is because it's dead wrong.

Not long ago, a stock market analyst covering the banking industry wrote in a note to his followers that when a bank caters to its customers it is wasting its money, diverting resources it should be applying elsewhere. According to the *New York Times,* the analyst, who already had a rather contrarian reputation, said banks should keep their focus on the all-important central task of pushing products and managing risk, even if it meant neglecting customer service.

Whether you find this idea appealingly counter-intuitive or not, the decision on whether to focus on the customer experience should never be a binary choice; the question is how much attention you should pay to it. Nor is your company's quarterly bottom line the sole indicator of financial success; long-term shareholder value is also important.

All businesses – including banks – create 100 percent of their bottom-line profit and shareholder value through serving customers. In the final analysis, if you don't have a paying customer then it doesn't matter how superb your products are or how skillfully you manage risk.

Without a customer, you don't have a business at all. You have a hobby.

Unfortunately, too many businesses still seem to embrace the idea that customers are essentially "service problems" to be resolved and served as inexpensively as possible. For a business following this reasoning, a customer is just an *object* – one more obstacle that lies between the business and a higher bottom-line profit. The more customers, the more obstacles to overcome and problems to deal with.

Just ask yourself how customer care is handled at your own company. Is the customer service budget shaved down as much as possible every year, in order to reduce your cost of doing business? Or is it treated as an investment designed to improve shareholder value?

The problem is that the real economic benefit of customer loyalty and retention isn't generally recognized in a firm's financial statements, because this value won't be realized until future periods. However, the *costs* of providing customer service must be recognized as they are incurred. So the more a business focuses on its current-period bottom line (as opposed to its long-term shareholder value), the more averse the business will likely be to customer-centric initiatives.

That's the message this contrarian bank analyst was trying to put across: that (at least to him) the short-term costs of delivering a better customer experience weren't worth the long-term benefits of increased customer loyalty and shareholder value.

But for the vast majority of businesses, customers are the primary link between short-term earnings and long-term shareholder value.

If you think about it, a customer is really just a bundle of future cash flows, with a memory. And these future cash flows will increase or decrease based on how the customer remembers being treated, today.

So for a bank, the mission should be to keep every customer's cash flow as positive as possible, while recognizing that (as they say in the investment business) past performance is no guarantee of future results.

Defining the "Customer Experience"

A lot of businesses are concerned with improving their customers' experiences. But before going too much further, we probably ought to define the term. What are the actual elements of a "customer experience," and what should you focus on? What kinds of actions would improve the experience you offer to customers?

In my view, any useful definition of "customer experience" should be based on straightforward language, while at the same time clearly differentiating the term from all the other marketing terms and buzzwords out there, such as customer service, brand preference, customer satisfaction, CRM, or customer loyalty.

So here's a simple definition of customer experience that is both straightforward and differentiated from other buzzwords.

> Customer experience is: *The totality of a customer's individual interactions with a brand, over time.*

Each of the terms in this definition is important, because each term identifies some aspect of your own company's customer experience that you have to pay attention to when it comes to making improvements. If you are crafting an initiative to improve your customer experience, the words in this definition will help ensure that you are focusing on the right things, and not undermining or diluting your effort:

- The word *"customer"* is meant to include both current and prospective buyers and users. When you make it easier for a prospect to find information about your firm or your product, for instance, you are improving the "customer experience" even though the prospect may never actually become a customer.

- *"Individual"* means that we are talking about each different customer's own individual perception or impression of the experience. What you intend to provide a customer is not nearly as important as how the customer perceives what you provide.

- *"Interactions"* occur in addressable or reciprocal channels, i.e., non-mass media. Marketing campaigns, taglines, and brand messages may be important, but they aren't interactions, so they lie outside the "customer experience» domain. On the other hand, improving your mobile app by, for instance, embedding voice or chat connections into it, would definitely improve your customer experience.

- *"With"* a brand means that only direct contact counts as part of the customer experience. The interactions a customer has with others *about* a brand are not really a part of it, although of course how your company actually *engages* with customers and prospects within various social channels is, because it is a direct interaction.

- *"Brand"* is a proxy for all your marketing, selling, and servicing entities. In addition to your own company, it includes dealers and distributors, marketing and advertising agencies, any retailers that sell your product, and any service firms that install or repair your company's product, or that handle customer inquiries or interactions of any kind. For each of these interactions, you can contract out the task, but not the responsibility – at least not as far as the customer is concerned.

- *"Over time"* recognizes the ongoing nature of a customer relationship. Each customer's experience is not an isolated event, but accumulates through time. You improve your customer experience, for instance, when you make it easier for a repeat customer to get back to their preferred configuration, or when your call center agent already knows what a prospect was just trying to find out on your web site.

- And the very first word in the definition, *"totality,"* means that you cannot improve your customer experience without considering all of these issues in total, including how each one impacts the others. Integrating your interaction channels may be the single most important step you can take today to improve your customer experience, and there are all sorts of new technologies now available to do this.

Customer Experience in a Diagram

What does it mean to be focused on your customer's experience, as a business? Assuming that you start with a quality product and service, focusing on the customer experience requires you to understand the customer's own point of view and respect the customer's interest. You must fix problems, handle complaints, and remember individual customer preferences.

But it isn't merely a matter of adding up these different components of quality, service, insight, and responsiveness, either. You can introduce all these ideas into your business model, but if you don't grapple with your company's most basic strategic objective, then sooner or later your efforts to focus on the customer experience will fail.

In the past I've found it helpful to explain the contrast between customer-centric and product-centric competition by using a diagram, illustrating visually that these two strategies actually represent different "dimensions" of competition. If you think about it, for a business to be competitively successful, it must meet two conditions:

- It must be able to satisfy a customer's need; and

- It must have a customer who wants to have that need satisfied.

The product-centric competitor focuses on one need at a time and tries to find as many customers as possible who want to have that particular need met, while the customer-centric competitor focuses on one customer at a time and tries to satisfy as many of that customer's needs as possible – across all the company's divisions and business units, and through time (i.e., meeting a customer's needs week after week, month after month).

If we visualize a kind of "marketing space" defined by the different customer needs a business can satisfy (the vertical dimension) and by the different customers it has (the horizontal dimension), then we can map customer centricity and product centricity on the same diagram:

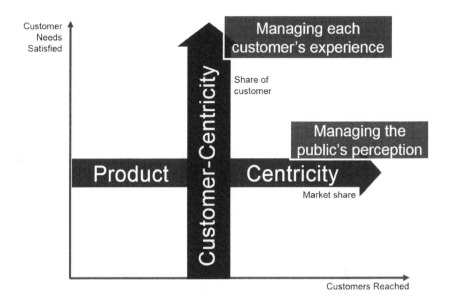

From this diagram it should be clear that customer centricity doesn't actually *conflict* with product centricity, because they aren't opposite in direction. They're orthogonal, so these two different types of competition have little or no effect on each other. That is, the strategies and tactics you follow to be more product-centric will have little effect on your share of customer, while customer-centric strategies will have little effect on your market share.

Both of these strategies are useful to a business. Both can be pursued simultaneously, and in fact most businesses *do* pursue these strategies simultaneously. It's important to acquire more customers for your business by promoting products and services that meet specific customer needs, but once you have gone to all the trouble and expense of acquiring a new customer, it's at least equally important to pay attention to keeping that customer longer, and satisfying even more of their needs.

But in addition, this graph illustrates the role that customer experience plays, because while a product-centric competitor focuses on managing the public's perception of the product (i.e., its brand image), a customer-centric competitor must focus on how it delivers each customer's individual experience.

There are, however, a few more points worth explaining in this diagram.

First, this two-dimensional marketing space is not defined by products, per se, but by different customer needs. So when you think about your "share of customer," you shouldn't just think in terms of wallet share. Instead, ask yourself what share of this customer's *needs* are you actually meeting? What share of this customer's *life* are you participating in? And, what *additional* products or services might allow you to increase your participation in the customer's life, overall?

Indeed, while product-centric competition involves finding more customers for the products you offer, customer-centric competition, at its best, involves finding more products to meet even more of the needs your customers have.

Second, unlike products, customers have memories. This means that the business customers generate for you tomorrow, either as a repeat customer or as a reference for other customers, will be based partly on their memory of how good their experience was today. Whether you remember them or not, customers remember you.

So focusing on the customer experience is a qualitatively different kind of competition than focusing on the product and its ability to attract more customers. Products don't have experiences, and they don't have memories. How you treat a product today has absolutely no effect on that product's value to you tomorrow. But your customer's experience today has everything to do with that customer's value to you tomorrow.

The implications of this final distinction are very important, because customers are the most direct link between the profit you make today and the profit you are likely to make tomorrow. The customer relationship directly connects today's profits and costs to your company's overall shareholder value.

What Kind of Customer Experience Are You Capable of Delivering?

From the definition of "customer experience," it's clear that delivering a better experience involves improving the quality both of a company's interactions with its customers and its individualized treatment of them.

But different businesses will have different capabilities when it comes to interacting and customizing. One company may be able to interact with individual customers only by phone, for instance, while another could also engage via email, online chat, or perhaps even real-time video. And in terms of the product or service it renders, one firm might have the ability to deliver different types of service to a few broad segments of customers, while another has the ability to track individual customers and to modify its service or offering as necessary to meet specific, individual customer demands.

So we can think of these two capabilities – interacting and customizing – as having a kind of scale, on which any individual business could be highly proficient or not so proficient. Your own company's mix of capabilities when it comes to interacting with, and customizing for, customers will actually define the kind of customer experience you're capable of delivering.

Below is a "Customer Experience Capabilities Matrix" outlining four different kinds of customer experience, based on a company's capacity for (1) cost-efficiently and effectively interacting with customers, and (2) customizing its behavior toward individual customers, based on who they are.

Customer Experience Capabilities Matrix

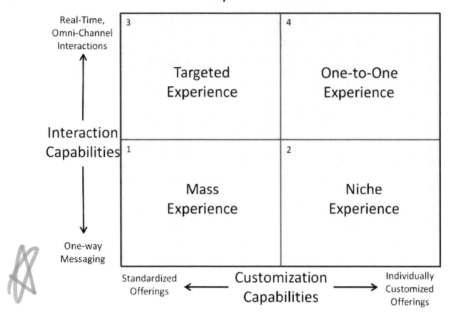

In Quadrant 1, on the lower left, a company that has little ability to either interact with individual customers or customize for them, will rely almost entirely on advertising and promotion, and its product or service offering will be fairly standard for all customers, delivering a "mass" customer experience designed to be pretty much the same for everyone. In the B2C space, think of Procter & Gamble selling Tide detergent to millions of customers with the same basic brand message. This kind of customer experience is less common in B2B selling, but it could describe the way some large enterprises sell into the small-and-medium business (SMB) market.

The "niche" customer experience delivered in Quadrant 2, on the lower right, is the result of a company that can alter its product in meaningful ways for different types of customers, but it isn't capable of interacting with those customers richly enough to be able to fit specific products to specific customers. Instead, it will market to different niches, using niche-specific one-way messaging. A typical brick-and-mortar chain of athletic shoe stores, for instance, might choose to offer one kind of customer experience to sports enthusiasts,

ıshion junkies. It lacks the capability,
ividual customers, in order to shape a

ıy has the reverse problem: it isn't capa-
ıct offering, but it does have the capabil-
individual customers. In this case, you
ind of "targeted" customer experience.
firm is interacting and communicating
individually, but the communication is not designed to elicit an individual
customer's needs so much as it is aimed at positioning and selling the product
that the company has available. Loyalty programs fall into this quadrant, for
the most part. Your typical airline loyalty program, for instance, will involve
you in a great deal of interaction with the airline, and you might earn enough
points to qualify for expedited check-in – but everyone qualifies in exactly
the same way, and on the flight itself there's no mad scramble for particular
seats or locations. (Airlines could increase their capability to customize if they
begin remembering your meal or beverage preference from one flight to the
next, or even if they just acknowledge your home city the next time they send
you a "fare sale" email blast.)

It is in Quadrant 4 that a company is capable of delivering a genuinely "one to
one" customer experience. If your business can interact efficiently with customers in real time, and also tailor your product-service offering for individual customers, then the experience you deliver to the customer will be more
meaningful for them and more profitable for you. When a customer interacts
with you to tell you how they want to be served, and you tailor *that customer's*
product or service to meet that specification, the relationship is now "owned"
by both of you.

In fact, when you deliver a truly one-to-one customer experience, you are pre-
disposing the customer to *want* to be loyal, rather than switch to a competitor.
Even if your competitor offers the same level of rich interaction and personal
customization, in order for your customer to get back to the same level of
convenience he now enjoys with you, he'd first have to spend time interacting
with your competitor to "re-specify" what he's already specified with you.

15

It is in Quadrant 4, with a one-to-one customer experience, that a business can realize the true benefits of managing relationships with customers.

It's important to note that companies and industries are not born into these quadrants. Yes, their business models might make it more or less difficult to improve their ability to interact and customize, but no matter where your own company falls in this matrix today, you merely have to improve your technical capabilities to move into Quadrant 4, and deliver a one-to-one customer experience.

CHAPTER 2

Customers Just Want Their Problems Solved

Like water or electricity, customers seek the path of least resistance.

Except on very rare occasions (an entertainment experience, for instance), customers don't buy from a company just for the enjoyment of it. They have problems to solve and needs to meet. They want these needs to be met and these problems to be solved as conveniently, inexpensively, and expeditiously as possible.

That's what customers are buying, and your customer experience needs to be designed, first and foremost, to satisfy this demand.

Take the Friction Out of Your Customer Experience

In physics, friction is the enemy of efficiency. It bleeds energy out of a machine or system, generating heat and noise. The Second Law of Thermodynamics (entropy always increases) means that some friction is inevitable, but the less friction a system generates, the better. Friction is a waste product, with very few redeeming attributes.

In a consumer's life, friction plays a similar role, bleeding energy out of the customer experience. The wasted time required to hold on the phone or to wait in the queue before speaking with a service rep is friction. Friction is the time and money spent getting an item repaired or replaced when it breaks or runs down. It is the cost of gasoline used, when driving to and from the store for groceries. Even the time and effort spent online trying to figure out which product is better, or which service package makes the most sense, constitutes friction.

But the inevitable existence of consumer friction also represents a business opportunity. Because every time you can reduce the friction in your customer's experience, you are adding value, eliminating waste. You are making the customer's life run more smoothly. So identifying and eliminating the kinds of friction your customer encounters can be very beneficial when it comes to gaining a competitive advantage and improving a customer's loyalty and lifetime value.

When Ally Bank clearly displays its toll-free number on every page of its website, along with the estimated wait time before speaking with a rep, it is adding value to your customer experience by eliminating friction. When JetBlue automatically credits your account with the value of a refund due to a delayed or canceled flight, it is removing friction from the customer experience. When Safelite AutoGlass emails you a picture of the repairman scheduled to come to your house on a service call, in advance of his arrival, the company is adding value by removing friction. And one of Amazon's latest friction-removing initiatives, according to CEO Jeff Bezos, will be to send a refund to a customer in advance of the customer even having to request it, whenever a service situation would normally call for one.

The highest quality customer experience is one that is as frictionless as possible. So what are some of the opportunities your own business might have to gain a competitive advantage by eliminating consumer friction? Here are just a few ideas to start your thinking:

- Simplify your pricing

- Reduce the complexity of your "terms and conditions," including privacy-protection assurances, refund requirements, warranty conditions, and other service rules

- Allow your customers to post product reviews on your own website, comparing brands without having to search elsewhere

- Improve your customer data system so that a customer never has to repeat information to you (everyone's favorite gripe: being required to key in their account number when they first connect with the contact center, and then when they finally talk to a live human, the first question is "what's your account number?")

- Design a smartphone app allowing customers to accomplish routine tasks without having to wait for your participation (depositing a check by emailing its photo, for instance, or locating your store, or checking on a package).

- Train and empower your service employees to make non-routine decisions on their own authority.

To both the physicist and the consumer, friction is the enemy. It may never be possible to totally eliminate it, but the less friction generated, the better.

The Best Customer Experience Is NO Customer Experience

All over the world, companies are trying to meet increasing customer expectations by improving their customer experience. Executives appoint Customer Experience Managers, they share their findings at customer experience conferences, they read books on customer experience management, and everyone genuflects reverently before the high altar of "CXM" (customer experience management).

Managing how customers experience your company's product or service has become a universal requirement for being competitively successful.

So, why would I have chosen such a provocative headline for this essay? Because there's actually a great deal of truth to the idea that customers aren't really looking for "experiences."

Think about your own business for a minute. Unless your name is Disney, your customers almost certainly aren't coming to you for the "experience" of buying from you. They're coming to you because they want to solve some problem or meet some need, and they think your company has a product or service that will help them do that – whether it's feeding the family a meal, or fixing their car, or maybe communicating with a friend.

And here's the thing: If they could solve their problem or meet their need without ever having to deal with your company (or any company) at all, don't you think they would do that?

What this means is that the ideal customer experience should be designed to be as easy and painless as possible. The ideal experience would be one that requires absolutely no extra effort on the customer's part. The customer would never have to repeat anything they'd already said, and no obstacles would have to be overcome in the process of meeting the customer's need. The more that a customer's experience with your product and service fades into the background, in fact, the faster and more conveniently the customer will be able to meet their need.

That's why my suggestion is that the *ideal* customer experience is *no* experience. In the *ideal* situation, the only thing a customer would "experience" would be the elimination of whatever need or problem drove them to you in the first place.

Marketing research supports this idea. Studies have consistently shown that customer loyalty is not very highly correlated with customer satisfaction scores, although customer disloyalty does have a high correlation with customer dissatisfaction. Matthew Dixon, Nick Toman, and Rick Delisi, for instance, in their 2013 book *The Effortless Experience*, cite a survey of some 97,000 consumers conducted by the Corporate Executive Board, which found "virtually no difference at all between the loyalty of those customers whose expectations are exceeded and those whose expectations are simply met...[and] virtually no statistical relationship between how a customer rates a company on a satisfaction survey and their future customer loyalty."

In fact, the survey found an R-squared (coefficient of determination) of just 0.13 between satisfaction and loyalty, which is very close to zero. (R-squared values range from 0 to 1.0, and to put this particular score into perspective, the R-squared correlation between "getting good grades in school" and "achieving career success later in life" is 0.71.)

To put it simply, customers don't necessarily stay because they're satisfied, but they often leave because they're not.

Across industry after industry, the key driver of customer disloyalty is dissatisfaction, driven by unresolved problems or service issues. From the customer's perspective, this represents friction, and the same study reports that a customer service interaction is roughly four times more likely to drive disloyalty than loyalty. That is, every time you interact with a customer, you are four times as likely to drive the customer away as to turn him into a raving fan.

So when you start journey-mapping your customers or trying to design a better customer experience, before brainstorming all the ways you can "surprise and delight" them, make sure you have eliminated as many problems and obstacles as possible, in order to make the experience easy, simple, and totally frictionless.

You want a customer experience so frictionless that the customer won't even notice it.

Are You Making It Hard for Customers to Buy From You?

Eliminating friction in the customer experience is really about obliterating all the obstacles and problems that customers encounter when they want to buy or use your product. Think of all the tasks a customer must accomplish in order to get your product or service to meet whatever need he or she has in mind. And then work to ensure that there are absolutely as few tasks as possible, and that they are as simple as possible.

If you look at a business – *your* business – from the customer's point of view, it really won't be difficult to identify such obstacles. But to make things simpler, I've put together a checklist of things you should be doing, in order to minimize friction:

On your website:

✓ Use standard navigation features

✓ Make sure phone numbers appear on every page

✓ Provide "talk to someone" or "chat" buttons throughout

✓ Provide "contact us" buttons making it easy to email your company, and be sure to specify how much time will likely be required before a reply is sent. Forms aren't enough.

At your call center:

✓ Try to answer as many calls as possible without requiring a customer to navigate a "phone tree" interactive voice response (IVR)

✓ Coordinate whatever IVR choices you must offer with the choices shown on your website

✓ Rely on short menus for your IVR, in order not to tax a customer's memory

✓ Provide options to leave a number (and a time) for callback

- ✓ Allow the customer to hit 0 at any point to reach a human representative

- ✓ Don't evaluate calls by their length – longer calls almost always provide more value to customers

On your outbound email campaigns:

- ✓ Be sure the subject line contains enough information to understand the reason for the email

- ✓ If you're emailing to alert the customers to an update requiring them to log in to your website, tell them something about the nature of the update in the email itself

- ✓ Provide direct links from the email message to whatever pages on your website correspond with the subject matter

- ✓ Always include a phone number in the email message

- ✓ List clearly the alternatives to using the website

At your stores, branches, or physical outlets:

- ✓ Provide phones for calling the contact center directly

- ✓ Make self-service desks available for information

- ✓ If you have an online offering (and you should), then equip your sales people with tablets to access it (your customers will already be using their smartphones to access your online offering, and possibly your competitors' offerings, as well)

Be proactive with your notifications to customers:

Contact the customer in the event of an unexpected problem or failure

Contact whenever necessary to protect a customer's best interest (credit card fraud, nearing the limit on a pricing plan, about to incur a late fee, and so forth)

Provide this and other information to the customer in a way he can control (choices with respect to alerts, frequency of contact, privacy controls, etc.)

Reach out to customers to manage their expectations appropriately whenever lengthy or time-consuming processes are involved

It's really very simple: If you want to eliminate friction, then you have to experience that friction from your customer's point of view.

Treating Different Customers Differently

Customers are all unique and different individuals, and one important component of a frictionless customer experience is relevance. You want to deliver to each different customer an experience that is relevant to him or her. Being relevant to any customer inherently implies treating that customer differently from how you treat other customers.

As it happens, "treating different customers differently" is also the single most concise definition of Customer Relationship Management, or "CRM." The actual process goes by many names – customer experience management, personalized marketing, customer centricity, customer intimacy, or one-to-one marketing. But whatever you call it, the process commences when you begin treating Customer A one way and Customer B another way, based on what you know about their differences, in order to improve each customer's experience and to make each of them more valuable to your business.

Before the advent of computer databases and interactivity, it wasn't practical to treat different customers differently. Unless you were a B2B seller, or perhaps a personal services firm with just a few large clients, you had to treat all your customers the same. To do anything else would have been just too costly. It was really the advent of the World Wide Web that generated what we now all recognize as the customer revolution, which has required every business to ask itself how to do a better and more efficient job of treating its different customers differently, whether it has thousands of customers, or tens of millions.

But how are customers different, actually? From a business perspective, there are really just two principal ways:

1. Customers have different values to the business, and

2. Customers have different needs from the business.

These two kinds of differences account for both sides of your value proposition: what your customers pay you, and what they want from you. All other descriptions of customer differences – segmentation models, transaction histories, demographics, and psychographics – are really just interim steps designed entirely to allow a business to infer the answer to these two questions: How much is this particular customer worth? And what does this particular customer want?

But note that these two descriptions will appeal differently to businesses and to customers. To most businesses, insight into a particular customer's *value* is clearly the highest priority. Companies thirst to know which of their customers are the most valuable, which would allow them to increase the efficiency of their marketing efforts. They can spend more on serving their most valuable customers (to try to retain them longer), while peppering them with more sales appeals (because they're more likely to buy).

The thing is, however, your customers really only care about the second difference – their *needs*. For the most part, customers don't know and don't care what their value is to you. They are concerned with what they need – what problem they want solved, what task accomplished, or what aspect of their own life improved.

And, different customers often have very different needs from the business. As difficult as it is analytically to differentiate your customers by their values, the fact is that the problem is one-dimensional. The answer can be expressed in dollars and cents. Or pounds and pence.

But there are as many different dimensions of customer needs as there are analysts and marketers to think them up – not just demographics and psychographics, but personality types, buying behaviors, social media participation, etc. Needs-based customer differentiation is really where the pay dirt is for CRM.

Please don't get me wrong here, because ranking customers by their value is indeed a necessary step in setting up a customer-centric marketing program. But while it's necessary, it's not sufficient for long-term success. It isn't likely to generate much customer goodwill or genuine emotional loyalty. And it will leave you vulnerable to competition from another company that can better tailor its own offerings to the more finely differentiated needs of your customers.

To create genuine loyalty you have to try to see your business through the customer's own eyes. You need to *be* the customer, to think the customer's own thoughts. And the customer won't be thinking about their value to your business. They'll be thinking about what they need from it.

The Real Implications of the 80-20 Rule

Imagine you had access to a baseball stadium full of 50,000 customers and prospective customers in your category. How would you go about increasing the amount of business you're getting from these customers?

Well, with a captive audience like this, locked into their stadium seats, you could put ads up on the lighted stadium board, or maybe sponsor some in-game announcements or contests. You might also put your logos on the seatbacks or the hotdog wrappers, or advertise on the billboards into and out of the stadium, or all of the above.

But the fact is that this isn't a very efficient use of resources. Because *some* of these customers will inevitably be much more valuable to you than others, and your marketing investment would be much more productive if you knew who they were.

The Pareto Principle, also known as the 80-20 rule, suggests that there is a skew to the value of your customers, and that 80 percent of your profit likely comes from just 20 percent of your customers. Of course, the actual magnitude of this skew is different in different kinds of businesses. For an airline it is probably as steep as a 90-10 distribution, while for a grocery store, say, it might be more like 70-30, or even shallower. Whatever skew applies, the result is a kind of "power law distribution" of values, and this is very different from your standard normal curve, or bell curve.

What some people forget about this kind of distribution is that if 20 percent of your customers do 80 percent of your business, then 20 percent of *that* top 20 percent will do 80 percent of that 80 percent, and so on. So, the top 5 percent or less of your customers will often account for two-thirds of your profit, and the top 1 percent may account for close to half of your profit all by themselves.

If your customer base has an 80-20 skew, in other words, then somewhere in this stadium full of 50,000 customers there may be 100 who do close to *more than half the amount of business done by the other 49,900 customers put together!*

So rather than paying to put your ad message in front of all 50,000 customers, with a series of stadium-wide initiatives, why wouldn't you invest a little of your marketing budget to find out where in the stadium these 100 people are actually sitting? Then you could hire some folks to go up into the stands, sit down next to each one of them, buy them a hotdog and a drink, and simply ask them what it would take to get more of their business. (And then, of course, you would do it!)

By the end of the game you would have taken more than half the market, and the entire process would have taken place completely outside of your competitors' view. This is the real power of direct, interactive marketing. One-to-one marketing. Customer-centric marketing. CRM.

Of course, the stadium is just a metaphor, and in the real world there's a lot more to it.

- **Analytics:** First, you'll need reliable and sophisticated analytics not just to rank your customers by their value but also to determine where and how you can interact with them individually (i.e., where are they "sitting in the stadium").

- **Interaction:** You'll also have to be able to conduct individual discussions with each customer in order to get their feedback (customer insight) regarding what it would take to earn more of their business.

- **Personalization:** And (last but probably the most difficult capability of all) you'll need to treat each of these different customers differently, tailoring your treatment of an individual customer to that particular customer's individual specifications, so you can pay off your promise of personalized service for each of them.

None of these capabilities is a slam-dunk. But if you want to set up and manage relationships with individual customers, it's best if you also know which particular customers are most worth the relationships in the first place.

CHAPTER 3

Every Customer's Experience Is Personal

A market is incapable of having an "experience" with your product or service. Markets and market segments, no matter how thinly sliced and carefully defined, do not use your product or service to meet some need. Markets and segments are inanimate. They have no intellect of their own, but are simply intellectual constructs, designed by thinking people to help other thinking people simplify complexity and make useful generalizations.

Only customers – human customers with awareness, feelings, and memories – are capable of "experiencing" the way you treat them. So one of the most important aspects of managing your customer experience is that you are trying to manage each customer's own, personal feeling about your product or service. You're trying to behave in such a way that each individual customer has a more positive *feeling* about what they experience with you.

But feelings, by their very nature, are unique and personal. A customer can share her feelings with another customer by talking about them, or blogging about them, or rating the company on a scale of one to 10. But no matter how much a customer shares in this way, in the end her own feelings will continue to be unique to her, and only imperfectly described by whatever method she chooses to describe them.

Different Customers Have Different Needs

LEGO sells great toys all over the world, and it knows that its customers "use" its products for different reasons. On any given day, in fact, three 10-year-old children might buy the same exact set of LEGO blocks in the same store for the same price, but for three completely different reasons:

- **Constructing**. The first child enjoys figuring out the diagrams that come with LEGO blocks and then putting things together exactly as specified.

- **Role playing**. The second child gets the most fun from putting a toy together and then pretending he is the spaceship captain or the race car driver for the toy he just built.

- **Creating**. The third child wouldn't dream of putting together something that someone else had already put in a diagram! She wants to see what else she can build that might be completely different.

The thing is, when LEGO knows which child is which, it can sell them a variety of other products and services to meet their different needs. For the "constructor" it can offer extra diagrams for more toys that can be put together from the same set of blocks, along with diagrams of things that can be constructed from multiple sets. For the "role player" it can sell costumes, accessories, story books and videos. And, for the "creator" it can offer imaginative challenges – pictures of other possible uses for the blocks, but without the blueprints, for instance.

We all know that when we sell to a customer we need to do it in such a way as to appeal to the customer's motivation, or *need*. But it's easy to forget that customers are all different, and their needs are often quite different as well.

At the most basic level, customers differ from each other in just *two* fundamental ways – their value to the business, and what they need from the business. All other descriptions of customers – demographics, product preferences, spending records – are aimed at capturing one of these two principle differences. And while it's important to understand which customers have the most value, which ones have the most growth potential, and which ones are perhaps not profitable at all, you won't be able to change any customer's behavior (to get them to stay loyal longer, or to buy more lines of product, say) unless you know what motivates them.

In order to achieve whatever objective you have with any particular type of customer, you have to change that customer's behavior, right? And how do you do that? How do you change a customer's behavior?

By appealing to the customer's own individual *needs*. By showing the customer how a behavior change can better satisfy whatever need or desire is motivating him.

The problem is that customer needs are multidimensional. They aren't denominated in dollars and cents, like customer value. And the only practical way to act on different customers' different needs is to simplify things by categorizing your customers into needs-based groups (such as LEGO's constructors, role players, and creators).

The best way to begin differentiating your customers by their needs, however, is to field some scientific market research, designed to cluster your customers around a multidimensional framework based on how different customers make various trade-offs against various personal desires, product features, or benefits.

Forrester's research in the telecom category clusters smartphone users in terms of whether they are technology optimists or pessimists, whether they have high or low income, and whether they use their phones primarily for family, business, or entertainment purposes. Based on this combination of factors, it describes the characteristics of various clusters of customers using colorful names such as "mouse potatoes," "gadget grabbers," "hand shakers," and "techno-strivers," among others.

In our consulting work, needs-based differentiation of customers is the secret to delivering a more relevant customer experience, so it is often one of the first tasks we tackle. Sometimes we can rely on generic, category-based research (like Forrester's, in the smartphone category), while other times we urge a client to conduct some original research. For a national online florist business, for instance, we identified customers who were:

- Well-meaning but overwhelmed (they need advice),

- Big-hearted benefactors (impulsive and indulgent),

- Practical and self-sufficient (sometimes they forget dates),

- Slow but sentimental (they want something imaginative and memorable), or

- Last-minute and lavish (they often forget dates, need help, and they're happy to spend).

But even before fielding this kind of market research, you may be able to make some useful judgment calls with respect to your customers' own different categories of needs. Here are a few "thought starters" to stimulate your creativity.

An international airline might serve:

- Utility and schedule buyers,

- Luxury and comfort seekers,

- Price shoppers and bargain hunters,

- Deal makers, or

- Insecure decision makers.

A commercial real estate business might encounter:

- Active deal makers (interested mostly in speed and flexibility),

- Buy-and-hold investors (interested in cost containment and operational efficiency), or

- Operators (interested in synergies, combinations, and ways to improve a property's value).

A truck-and-tire dealership would probably have customers who are either:

- Big fleet owners (who want consistency and convenience, and who treat speed-of-service and cost-of-service as interchangeable values),

- Mom-and-pop operators (who value friendliness and trust, and want to make "deals"), or

- Specialty vehicle firms (tank trucks, refrigerated vehicles, flatbeds, etc.).

Note that all these distinctions are inherently artificial and approximate. They are not exact, and they never could be exact, because customers are individuals, not categories. But they are useful as generalizations, precisely because they simplify a very complex notion and make it actionable.

In Customer Relationships, Context Is King

Hmaun binegs are craetrues of cnotxet. In fcat, cntxoet is the olny way we are albe to raed. As lnog as the fsrit and lsat lrettes of wrdos are in thier prpoer pleacs, not much else rllaey mttares.

Seeing things in context is one of the most important features of human intelligence, and it plays a vital role in our relationships with others, including the relationship that a customer has with a company. By focusing on deepening the context of your customer relationships, you can ensure greater customer loyalty and probably higher margins, as well.

Start with the fact that all relationships are inherently interactive, by definition. Relationships involve communication back and forth between two parties, and we expect the other party to respond and react to our input just as we respond and react to theirs. When a relationship develops a deep context, the interactions become more efficient. I can say less and less, but because of our previous interactions (i.e., the context of our relationship) you'll understand more and more.

When a customer tells you how she likes her product configured or delivered, for instance, and you remember her preferences when she buys again, you are using the context of the relationship to save time and trouble both for her and for your firm. Context streamlines the interaction when you rent a car and don't have to stop at the counter to fill out another contract from scratch, or when you use your bank's online bill paying service, so you don't have to re-enter each vendor's details every time you send a payment.

But to be competitively successful, you should go beyond simple descriptive and transactional data if you can, because the deeper the context of a customer relationship, the stronger it will be. What if your customers could specify their preferred sizes, colors, added features, and other product configuration details, along with their preferred delivery times? What if they could specify how often they want to be communicated with, how much additional warranty coverage they prefer, or what day of the month they prefer to be invoiced? Or what if your product itself were embedded with information technology allowing it to "recognize" a customer and remember the customer's previous settings in order to conform itself to their use more and more individually?

A deeper relationship context will improve a customer's loyalty by eliminating friction from the customer experience. It makes it more *convenient* for a customer to stay loyal, rather than to incur the friction of having to start from scratch with a different provider.

Relationship context is also the most reliable way to maintain your margins, because when your offer is individualized it is no longer simply a commodity. The customer herself has collaborated with you to create the most unique and valuable product-service configuration for her. So essentially, the service you are now providing was jointly created.

Developing context-rich relationships with customers requires you to start with the objective of treating different customers differently, and then to zero in on identifying and remembering the different preferences that individual customers have. This may sound particularly difficult if you've come to think of your product or service as commodity-like, with competition taking place largely in terms of price and promotion. But even for the most commodity-like of products, there will still be differences in the way customers perceive, desire, and use the product.

Here are a few questions you could ask yourself, in order to uncover potential context-building differences among your customers:

- How might different customers prefer your product in terms of its features or capabilities, size and fit, weight, color, design, style, timing, or frequency?

- What do different customers do differently with your product?

- How might different customers prefer the invoicing to be done, or the packaging, palletization, promotion, communication, or service support?

- Can you save your customer time or effort by remembering some detail or specification?

- What additional tasks does your customer have to accomplish to gain use out of your product, and what role could you play in helping them to accomplish these tasks?

- Are there particular types of customers with more complex problems or management issues?

- What ancillary services do your customers need in conjunction with your product?

To the extent you can actually deliver different services or offerings to meet some of these different needs, you can use this process to create loyalty.

Uncvoeirng tehse dffireneces and rmebemrieng tehm for eervy cutsmeor alolws you to depeen the cnotxet of yuor rleoitanhsips, one cutsmeor at a tmie.

Service or Cost? You Decide

In 1906, British physicist J.J. Thomson was awarded the Nobel Prize for his discovery that the electron is a particle.

In 1937, British physicist George Thomson, J.J.'s son, was awarded the Nobel Prize for showing that the electron is a wave.

So which is it, a particle or a wave? The correct answer is "both."

"Wave-particle duality" is one of the bedrock principles of quantum physics. Quantum physics, in turn, explains how transistors work, and transistors give us iPhones, word processing, GPS, and LinkedIn.

More than a decade ago I met with executives at Australia's St. George Bank, now part of the WestPac Group. At the time, St. George Bank had just reprogrammed its cash machines to "remember" an individual customer's usual transaction. When you put your cash card into a St. George Bank ATM and enter your PIN code, the ATM will ask, "Would you like your usual $100 cash withdrawal, no receipt?" This kind of personalization is more common today, but St. George Bank was one of the first to offer it, and it was extremely innovative at the time.

That morning in Sydney, the marketing executives I met with clearly recognized that their bank's innovation represented a greatly improved customer experience. And survey results showed that customers did indeed appreciate the initiative.

But then in the afternoon I met with some of the bank's senior IT executives. I complimented them on the fact that they had successfully implemented this highly customer-centric innovation, and I told them how much their marketing people appreciated being able to treat customers individually, remembering their preferences, and how happy they were about this improved customer experience.

I'll never forget what one of the IT executives said then. He scoffed at the very idea that this had been done to improve customer service. "That's not why we did this! Is that what the marketing people told you? Pfff! No way."

"Why did you do it, then?" I asked.

"We did it because real estate for ATMs in Sydney, Australia, is very costly, and new sites are difficult to come by. But this way, each of our ATMs serves many more customers in the same amount of time."

So which is it? Customer service, or increased business efficiency?

The correct answer is "both." Call it "friction-cost duality." When you use technology to deliver more humanity to customers and remove friction from the experience, your costs will go down, as well. Not only will customers be happier on account of the more personalized service, but you'll waste less time and effort on your side. This might mean better asset utilization (as St. George Bank found), or it could be reduced inventory carrying costs (if, for instance, you were mass customizing a product).

The point is that when you use computers to personalize each customer's experience, there is less wasted effort on both sides of the transaction. Your *customer* doesn't waste time and energy re-inputting information or specifications that he's already provided you, and your *business* doesn't waste time and effort offering every customer every option every time.

Relationships Will Be Required

Are you your customer's enemy?

Do you remember your customers individually, from one transaction to the next? Because if you don't – if your business has no memory of a customer's history with you – then every individual buying transaction is a self-contained, zero-sum game. You and your customer are in fact *enemies*.

Yes, you heard that right. You and your customer are adversaries with diametrically opposed interests, no matter how much you may try not to act the part.

Think about it: Your customer's goal for each individual purchase event will be to buy the most product at the lowest price from you, while your goal will be the exact opposite of this: to sell the least product at the highest price. Every dollar you gain is a dollar the customer had to give up, and vice versa.

If, on the other hand, you are able to remember individual customer interactions and transactions over time (either with the aid of computer technology or by using your own memory), then you are much more likely to *collaborate* with your customer to design just the right product, service, and overall customer experience this time around. "Let's see, last time we did it like this, so this time...?"

Whether it's a car rental company remembering your contract details so you don't have to fill out another form or a Starbucks barista remembering the way you like your latte, it will be a better customer experience. The more you remember about your customer, including their likes and dislikes, the richer "context" your relationship will have. And a deep relationship context is one of the most powerful keys to customer loyalty.

Do you want your customers to trust you, rather than to suspect your motives? Do you want them to consider you a reliable friend, rather than an adversary? There are a variety of strategies for achieving this objective, based on delivering a richer, more context-laden customer experience, so that a purchase transaction is no longer considered an isolated, zero-sum event.

But what this means is that you simply can't deliver a truly frictionless customer experience unless you have the tools and capabilities to develop and manage individual customer relationships, one customer at a time.

Four Steps to Managing Customer Relationships

In order to set up and manage your relationships with individual customers, you have to accomplish four basic tasks:

- **Identify** customers individually. Obviously, relationships are individual. You can't have a "relationship" with an audience or a population or a market segment, only with a single, individual customer. So before you can establish a relationship you must be capable of identifying your customers, one customer at a time. You don›t have to have each customer›s name and address, but you need to know that the customer on the phone right now is the same customer who was in the store yesterday, or on your website the day before that.

- **Differentiate** customers, one from another. Customers differ from each other, in terms of both their value to your business, and what they need from your business. Of course, you can't ever know what a customer really needs from you, or why he or she is buying, because you're not a mind reader. You can only infer what the customer needs by observing the customer's behavior. And the customer's behavior will then create (or destroy) value for your business.

- **Interact** with customers. Almost by definition, a relationship depends on some interaction between two parties. You want those interactions to be cost-efficient, so you need to drive them into more efficient channels. But you also want them to be *effective* – that is, to tell you something about the customer's needs or value that you can't learn simply by observing the customer's behavior.

- **Customize** for customers. The "pay off step" for managing a customer relationship comes when your business behaves differently toward that individual customer, based on what you know about them. We call this step "customization" even though we're not necessarily talking about it literally in terms of customizing the product or service. But whenever you treat Customer A differently from Customer B, based on what you think you know about their differences, you are "customizing" the customer's treatment.

If you've ever studied Customer Relationship Management ("CRM") academically, there's a good chance that these four steps – identify, differentiate, interact, and customize – are already familiar to you. Martha Rogers and I have produced two editions of a CRM textbook for graduate-level business students, *Managing Customer Relationships: A Strategic Framework*, and this textbook is organized around the "I-D-I-C" methodology. (And as I write these lines, we're starting work on a third edition). At our consulting firm, Peppers & Rogers Group, a large proportion of the work we do can be understood in terms of dissecting how these tasks work (or don't work) within a client's organization.

But a couple of other things are worth pointing out about the I-D-I-C model of relationship management. The first two tasks – identifying customers and differentiating them – are steps that a company can take within company walls. Your company has a database of individual customer records, you track the transactions and interactions of individual customers, and yet the customer herself never actually participates in the process. The customer may not even be aware of the data you are compiling, or the analysis you are doing.

By contrast, the third step – interaction – demands the customer's personal attention and participation. You can't interact with a customer unless the customer interacts with you, right? And ditto with the fourth step, customizing your behavior. This is the experience you deliver to a particular customer. It's called an "experience" because the customer experiences it. It involves the customer directly, as a participant.

So, you could think of the first two steps of the I-D-I-C model as "analytical" CRM, while the next two steps are "operational" CRM. Analytical CRM is required to develop better *customer insight*, while operational CRM is how you deliver a specific *customer experience*.

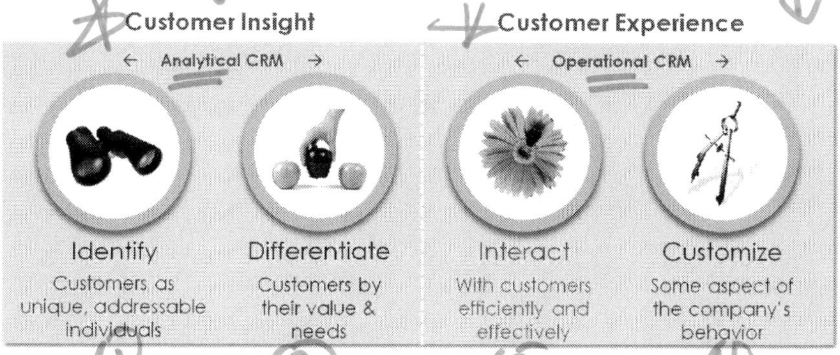

Handwritten annotations:
within co. walls ↓
IDIC
cust. involved ↓

Customer Insight | **Customer Experience**

← Analytical CRM → | ← Operational CRM →

Identify ① | Differentiate ② | Interact ③ | Customize ④

Customers as unique, addressable individuals | Customers by their value & needs | With customers efficiently and effectively | Some aspect of the company's behavior

If you think about the process of managing your own customers' individual relationships with your firm – through your website, your loyalty program, your contact center, at the point of purchase, or in after-sale service, virtually everything your company does can be understood in terms of how these four I-D-I-C steps are executed.

Delivering a better customer experience requires developing and managing relationships with your individual customers, and managing relationships requires the I-D-I-C process.

Brands Aren't the Same as Customer Relationships

You cannot have a customer relationship with a population of customers, or with an audience, or with a market segment. You can only have a *relationship* with an individual customer. Sometimes this point can be difficult to absorb, but the very idea of a customer "relationship" only makes sense when you're talking about one customer at a time.

In a workshop once, I was explaining the I-D-I-C model for understanding customer relationship management (CRM) – identify customers, differentiate them, interact with them, and customize for them.

At one point a brand manager in the workshop audience insisted that her brand's mission was to maintain a personal relationship with each of her customers. Part of her brand's role, she said, was to embody the relationship each of her customers had with the company. That's what she spent her time doing, she insisted – maintaining her individual customers' relationships with her brand.

But, no offense intended to brand managers anywhere, this is just not correct. It's entirely the wrong way to think about what a brand does.

Before going further, let me say that the brand plays a vital role in nearly every company's marketing success, as we are all increasingly bombarded with a cacophony of overlapping and conflicting commercial messages. Simply differentiating what one company's offering "stands for" in comparison to others' offerings is part of a brand's important role. A good brand is an extremely valuable asset *especially* today, when there is so much information inundating us.

However, differentiating your business is not what a relationship is about. A relationship involves differentiating your *customers* – which will then allow you to treat different customers differently. A relationship, by definition, involves direct, one-to-one interaction with an individual customer – a customer whose needs are different from the needs of other customers, and who will be treated differently as a result of his or her relationship. But brands don't interact with customers individually; they don't even know individual customers' identities. Brands do not treat different customers differently.

So I told the brand manager that her brand had basically the same kind of "relationship" with each of her customers as Justin Bieber had with my teenage daughter. My daughter had a picture of Justin on her wall, and she knew every one of his songs pretty much by heart. But Justin Bieber doesn't know who my daughter is, has never interacted with her, and has never changed his behavior in any way on the basis of what she said to him. If he did any of those things, then *that* would be a relationship.

If you want your business to be customer-centric, you need to know how profound the difference is between how your brand works and how a customer relationship works. Yes, having a well-respected brand can *help* you strike up relationships with your customers, because the customers will be more willing to engage with you because of your brand. And yes, having great individual customer relationships will in fact strengthen the brand, as well.

But relationships and brands operate in different marketing dimensions.

Brands aren't relationships. And relationships aren't brands.

What Honeybees Teach Us About the Customer Experience

Honeybees are social insects.

Whenever a foraging honeybee comes across a new flower rich in nectar, it returns to the hive and does a little "waggle dance" to tell all the other bees where to fly in order to find the bonanza. The honeybee waggle dance has been shown to be sophisticated enough that it accurately communicates not only the direction to the food source from the beehive, relative to the sun, but its distance from the hive, and even its overall attractiveness.

So imagine, for a moment, that your business is a flower, and that business success comes from providing nectar to the honeybee market. As the business manager in charge of this flower, your job is to generate the highest possible market share for your nectar. You want lots of individual bee visits in order to maximize the chances that your pollen will be spread to other flowers.

Occasionally, a bee buzzes through the airspace above you. How should you entice this potential customer to come take a look? Obviously, you do it with bright colors and an attractive smell.

But once you entice a bee to come in to sample your nectar, what determines whether that bee returns to the hive and spreads the word to all the other bees? That's simple: It's only going to do its waggle dance if it has judged your nectar good enough to merit telling everyone else.

Moral of the story: To encourage customers to sample your product, all you need is advertising. Bright colors and a great smell will get any single honeybee's attention at least long enough to make a visit. But if you want your customers to spread the word and come back for more, then you better provide a satisfying *customer experience*, as well.

Because in the end it isn't the attractiveness of your flower but the quality of your nectar that will entice a real swarm of customers to come in.

Human beings are social animals, also. We like being with others, telling stories, whispering rumors, playing games, laughing, entertaining, and being entertained. We like to share ideas, get feedback, discuss nuances, and sharpen our own thinking with other people's perspectives. We even look to others in order to know what our own true feelings should be. Being social is an essential ingredient of human nature. The term "antisocial" is an indictment, implying that someone is unfriendly, cold, or misanthropic. If you're antisocial, something must be wrong with you.

As important as our social nature is, however, social media and other interactive technologies have injected it with steroids. Before our very eyes, and within just the last 20 years or so, we have been transformed into a dynamic and robust network of electronically interconnected people in a worldwide, 24/7 bazaar of creating and sharing, critiquing, collaborating, helping, learning, competing, and having fun. We are like honeybees with smartphones, constantly doing our waggle dances on Pinterest, in the Twittersphere, or on the Facebook timeline.

It takes good marketing and advertising as well as a good customer experience to build any business into a success. You can't grow and prosper unless your marketing campaigns deliver a steady stream of new customers. But you also have to be sure these customers are in fact satisfied with the customer experience you deliver. And the more social your customers are – the more they communicate and interact with each other – the more important the customer experience becomes, relative to marketing and advertising.

Interactive technology has made delivering a better customer experience more vital to every company's success than ever before. And, as that technology continues to improve, the relative importance of the customer experience also increases.

Research by Google[1], in fact, does show a distinct and dramatic rise in the volume of social interactions that surround individual buying decisions. In just two years, for instance, the percentage of consumers who say they consult the opinions of their friends and connections prior to making a purchase nearly doubled, from 19 percent to 37 percent.

And guess what? When customers ask their friends about a product, they aren't asking about the advertising. They're asking about the customer experience.

They want to see the waggle dance.

What Do Your Friends Think?

Trust is our most important tool for evaluating incoming information and deciding what's important. Trust is how we decide what's worth our attention.

And the more technology continues to connect us with others, accelerating the incoming torrent of information, the more important trust becomes, because trust is what makes interactions efficient. Trying to deal with some person or company or information that we don't trust is a hassle. And the faster our lives go, the more of a hassle it is.

But our decision to trust someone or something is also influenced by our social relationship with others. One of the quickest ways for me to assess the trustworthiness of someone else, or of the information provided by someone else, is to see how my friends or associates assess them. I already trust my friend, or my business colleague, and if they vouch for it, then it's one less decision I have to make.

In business, a crude form of this vouch-safe process is the current practice of hosting customer reviews. By reading what others have already said about a product or company, I can get a better perspective on the quality of the customer experience I'm likely to have, rather than having to rely on what the company says about itself. And a whole host of third-party sites, from Angie's List to TripAdvisor to Yelp, have found business opportunities by making customer opinions available to other customers in a range of categories.

But in your real-world social life, you naturally trust some friends' opinions more than others. For instance, you might trust Adam's opinion when it comes to electronic equipment or high-tech things, but you wouldn't trust him to recommend the best sushi or Thai restaurant. You'd much rather know Becky's view on that. The problem with most customer review sites is that you are reading the opinions of complete strangers, with no way to assess their actual value.

In addition, sometimes the reviews themselves are fake. An unscrupulous business can pay shills to write bogus, glowing reviews of their products. There are tons of people selling this service online for a few pennies a word. So if you're a business with no principles, you can buy dozens of positive reviews for yourself and negative reviews for your competitors and flood the review sites with them.

A few years ago, for instance, the UK's Advertising Standards Authority questioned TripAdvisor's objectivity because of the prevalence of fake reviews. According to an article in *The Telegraph* newspaper, the crackdown "follows a complaint last year from two unnamed hoteliers and a website called Kwikchex, which helps companies manage their online reputations...Chris Emmins, co-founder of Kwikchex, said that there are a 'substantial' number of fake reviews on TripAdvisor, which is being 'abused by fraudsters.' Fake comments range from unsubstantiated claims of food poisoning in restaurants to theft and credit card fraud in hotels," said Mr. Emmins.

Forward-thinking sites (like Amazon, for instance) try to boost the trustworthiness of reviews by verifying whether a reviewer has actually bought the product (on Amazon), and by facilitating reviews of the reviewers. That's a big step in the right direction, but it requires a great number of reviews to make a "review the reviewer" system work, and not all businesses are as maniacally customer-focused as Amazon.

Increasingly, however, we will see the rise of "social filtering" – that is, filtering others' opinions based on the extent to which you know them. Rather than relying on the opinions of complete strangers, people will look to the opinions of their personal friends and colleagues, or even the friends of their friends.

Facebook's Graph Search application was a step in that direction (although a hesitant step, and probably not really aimed at the customer benefit of social filtering). *Fast Company's*[2] assessment of Graph Search's potential, for instance, included the suggestion that "The promise is that you'll find answers to queries that might stump Google, such as... 'friends of friends who like my favorite band and live in Palo Alto' or 'Indian restaurants in Palo Alto that friends from India like.'"

And there is already a growing assortment of social aggregators trying to harness this capability from a customer's existing network of online social connections. Wajam, TagWhat, and others now let you check what your connections have had to say about various products. I have a Wajam extension on my Chrome browser, and whenever I go online to check out a movie, or a restaurant, or a particular new product, if any of my connections have had anything at all to say about it, I'll have their comment flagged for my attention.

All this just serves to underscore the steadily rising importance of the customer experience to any business' success. If your customers have problems with the experience you give them, then that's the opinion they'll freely share with their friends. Not to get back at you, but simply to help their friends.

Because that's what friends do. They trust each other.

CHAPTER 4

Eliminate the Friction in Your Customer Experience

In physics, friction is mostly just waste. Friction simply adds to the increasing and inevitable randomness of the universe we live in – entropy.

For a customer, friction consists of wasted time, effort, or energy. Every time you task a customer with doing something that you could have done for him, it's just friction, from the customer's standpoint. It is waste.

So, if you want to know *how* to improve your customer's experience, then the very first thing you should concentrate on is eliminating friction.

The Shoe Salesman's Secret Motivation

One Saturday afternoon at a shopping mall during the busy Christmas season, a management consultant colleague of mine ventured into an athletic shoe store to buy some new running shoes. This particular consultant actually specialized in retail. He consulted both for retailers trying to improve their operations, as well as for manufacturers trying to sell their wares to retailers and retail chains. So whenever he went out on his own to buy anything he was always an observant shopper.

He told me that the shoe store seemed to be especially busy that afternoon, so he took a place in line behind two other folks being helped by one of the sales clerks. And as he waited, he saw that the salesman offered the same off-brand to each of these customers – customers who looked like they would have been willing to pay full price for a better name. The first customer, he said, had been interested in a pair of Nike basketball shoes, but the salesman first brought out this off-brand, at about half the price of the Nikes, and the customer ended up buying them. The same sales process, with the same result, ensued with the next customer, a woman who originally had said she was interested in the Reebok cross-trainers. But the salesman again talked the customer into trying out the cross-trainers from this off-brand first, and *she* bought them.

After watching two sales snatched from the jaws of well-known national brands, the consultant's curiosity was aroused. So when it was his turn to buy, he first asked the salesman why he had switched the two previous customers to this particular off-brand – a brand he'd never even heard of. After all, the consultant said, these customers seemed to have been willing to pony up higher prices for the name brands.

Oh, the salesman replied, it had nothing to do with margin or pricing, nothing at all. But he seemed a bit nervous at having been found out, and so my friend persisted. Was this off-brand paying some kind of bonus commission, then? Or was there some kind of contest or promotion going on? No, the salesman said. No, that wasn't it.

Then the clerk gestured toward all the people crowded into the store on this very busy afternoon. Look around, he said. See how busy it is in here? I don't even have time to slip away for a coffee or a bathroom break on a day like this, that's how crowded it is!

But this particular off-brand? Whenever they ship *their* shoes to the store, the laces are already in them, so it saves the clerk a lot of time not to have to lace up one of the other brands.

It seems to me that this little story is a perfect metaphor for illustrating the power of removing friction in your customer experience. That's what this off-brand shoe was doing. Their customer was the shoe store, and they were removing friction in their customer experience by lacing their shoes up in advance.

No matter what your business is, do you try to ship your shoes with the laces already in? Could you?

- If you're a retail bank, and your customer comes to you for a second mortgage, you could lace up the customer's shoes simply by filling out all the information on the mortgage application that your bank already knows about the customer (starting with name, address and bank account number!).

- If you're an airline and a flight gets canceled, you could lace up customers' shoes by re-booking them on the most likely flight immediately, and then texting or emailing them the information, rather than simply telling them the flight is canceled and requiring them to call in to re-book themselves.

- If you're a mobile phone company you could lace up a new customer's shoes by printing out a sample bill, while they're in your store or signing up for their service, so they can see what it's likely to cost, including all those charges that you don't like to mention.

Friction is the enemy of a good customer experience. Eliminate the friction and you're on your way to having a satisfied and loyal customer.

Four Attributes of a Frictionless Customer Experience

"Customer experience" is definitely a business buzzword these days. Customer Experience Management ("CEM") is all the rage in many marketing discussions, and everyone wants to deliver a better experience for their customers.

But what does that mean, really? What makes a customer experience better?

To answer that question, which lies at the heart of many, if not most, marketing strategies, you have to take the *customer's* perspective. And from the customer's point of view an excellent customer experience is one that is simply *frictionless*. No customer wants to be required to go to any extra trouble, or to fix problems, or to repeat things already communicated. The best kind of experience a customer can have is one in which he can meet his need or solve his problem completely effortlessly, without having to jump through hoops or overcome obstacles. Obstacles are friction. No one has time for obstacles.

To remove friction, marketers should focus on four basic attributes of a frictionless customer experience:

Reliability. Your product or service should perform as advertised, without failing or breaking down. You should answer your phone, your website should work, service should be performed on time, and so forth. Reliability in a customer experience is what you could call "product competence." A company's production and service processes must be *competent*. This means rendering a product or service on schedule, seamlessly across multiple channels and consistently through time, in such a way that it doesn't need a lot of maintenance, repair, correction, or undue attention from a customer to meet the customer's need.

Value. No one likes to be ripped off, which is what happens when you find out you've paid more for a product or service than it's worth. A frictionless customer experience is one in which the value-for-money relationship is appropriate. As a customer, when you go to Costco you don't expect a Bergdorf experience. But when you buy a Lexus, you expect more than a Ford experience. Whatever product or service you're buying must be good value-for-money. It will be economical for customers who are interested in price, and it will provide "fair value" for customers more interested in quality, status, or other attributes.

Relevance. If reliability is about product competence, then relevance is about "customer competence." The overwhelming majority of companies operating today are just not very customer competent. *Many* companies fail to remember their customers' details. Every time you have to tell a call center agent your account number again, having just punched it in on your phone, you are face to face with a company's customer incompetence. Customer incompetence is friction, and the most efficient way to overcome it is to remember each customer's individual specifications and needs, once you learn them.

Trustability. In today's hyper-interactive world, mere trustworthiness – that is, doing what you say you're going to do and not violating the law – is no longer sufficient to render a frictionless customer experience. Increasingly, customers expect you to be *proactively* trustworthy, or "trustable." A trustable customer experience is one in which the customer knows the company provides complete, accurate and objective information, and will help the customer avoid mistakes or oversights. If a customer has to count his change or double-check that he isn't doing something he's going to regret later, the experience is a hassle. It isn't frictionless. Some good markers of a trustable customer experience include facilitating objective customer reviews, or reminding a customer that the warranty period is nearly up, or advising customers when they're buying more than they need. Some companies (AOL, Vonage, Stamps.com, etc.) make it very difficult to quit your subscription. This is untrustable behavior, guaranteed to generate friction.

As business leaders, we all want to ensure that our products and services are positioned and delivered in such a way that customers receive an excellent customer experience. And from the customer's perspective, the less friction generated, the better that experience will be. It's really that simple.

Delivering a Reliable Customer Experience

If a frictionless customer experience is reliable, valuable, relevant, and trustable, then what does it mean to deliver a genuinely "reliable" customer experience?

A customer experience is reliable in the eyes of customers if it directly and efficiently solves their problem without introducing a host of other hassles, problems, or issues. You could think of reliability as a form of "product competence," because the word itself implies that customers can rely on the product to competently meet their needs.

Reliability not only involves the quality of whatever physical product might be sold to a customer, but also the efficiency of the services that surround that product – such things as handling inquiries and requests in a timely fashion, proficiency in making repairs or service improvements, and protecting your customers' data and privacy.

Start with the fact that customers don't think in terms of departments or silos. A company that delivers its customer experience through the separate, uncoordinated activities of two or three or a dozen different operating entities isn't likely to appear very reliable to the customer. Remember, it's the customer's perspective that defines the experience.

Regardless of whatever internal elements are involved in running your business, a reliable customer experience can only be delivered by removing the internal focus and division between "customer-facing" and "non-customer-facing" groups and processes to deliver a single, unified experience to each customer. From billing and invoicing to technology implementations and employee training programs, all parts of a company should consider their role in influencing the customer experience.

Take, for example, the case of a hospital client we once worked with. Its goal was to improve the patient experience in its Emergency Services Department ("ESD") by making its emergency room experience more reliable. Unfortunately, because of years' worth of bureaucratic requirements and compound, duplicated processes, the admissions procedure in the hospital's emergency room had grown to a mind-boggling 111 separate steps.

By focusing largely on a number of duplicative back-office operational processes, our client was able to make significant improvements. Using process mapping, detailed data analysis, and a review of current care delivery models, a team of hospital professionals collaborated to define new, integrated workflows. This resulted in a better, more reliable process for emergency room patients, as well as a more unified and collaborative environment within the ESD itself.

And the results were startling: Not only was the 111-step admission process cut to just 46 steps, trimming admission times by 14 percent, but most importantly for the patient, the time between arrival and seeing a physician was reduced by nearly 90 percent – from 27 minutes to just 3 minutes!

By focusing on product competence, in other words, this hospital not only boosted its own operating efficiency, but dramatically improved the *reliability* of the patient experience, as well.

Even luxury products and experience-based services can improve their customer experience by focusing on reliability and product competence. Consider the luxury resort and hotel space, for instance. As a very frequent international business traveler myself, I've had the privilege of sampling a large number of luxury hotels in a variety of countries over the last 20 years.

But I'll never forget how the Four Seasons Hotel Istanbul at the Bosphorus checked me in for a four-day stay during one business conference I attended a decade ago. Not only were my keys and check-in papers already waiting for me when I arrived, but the desk clerk asked me what time I would prefer to have my room cleaned each morning. And sure enough, the clean-up staff arrived every day at almost exactly that time.

More than simply a luxury experience, however, this added feature of the customer experience at the Four Seasons Hotel reassures the customer that the hotel is in fact reliable, and that its systems, processes, and products are *competent*.

Each customer has his or her own personal customer experience with your company. And, as in the saying, the beauty of that experience is in the eyes the beholder. So if you want to deliver a truly frictionless customer experience, start by re-imagining your processes from the perspective of the customer, and then make sure that they combine to provide the most reliable experience possible.

Price Is What You Pay. Value Is What You Get.

In the 19th century, a wagon-maker had to leave his shop in the care of his teenage son for a few days as he journeyed to a nearby town on business. Unsure of how to handle customers, the boy protested, "But Father, I don't know how much to charge for one of our wagons! What if I make a mistake?"

But the father replied, "It's easy, son. When someone asks 'how much for a wagon?' you say '$20.' If they don't blink at that, you say 'for the wheels.' And if they still don't blink, you say 'each.'"

Today's technologies are giving new life to this wagon-maker's pricing strategy. Financial services firms price their products based on a customer's reported income or wealth, and e-commerce sites charge a customer less if the customer lives near a competitive store. Supermarket chains are increasing their profits and generating more customer loyalty by charging individualized prices based on different customers' previous purchases.

As Warren Buffett said once, "Price is what you pay. Value is what you get."

A frictionless customer experience must be reliable, valuable, relevant, and trustable. But when considering the issue of value we have to think about a great deal more than just price.

Value represents the total utility or usefulness delivered to a customer, but it is an inherently subjective quantity. Price is an objective quantity. You can write it down or divide it into percentages. But value, like so much of the customer experience, is completely in the eye of the beholder. Something has value for me if I say it does.

So while we may not want to follow the wagon-maker's advice completely, there is some truth to the parable, and there's a lesson for us. The value customers perceive in your product or service bears a direct connection to the importance or urgency of whatever subjectively understood need they have for it. And since customers have different opinions about these needs, they will have different opinions about the value of your offering.

We know this to be true, for the simple reason that those who consider the value of your offering to be higher than its price are going to buy it, while those who consider its value lower than the price will not.

So in delivering value to a customer, the trick once again is to treat different customers differently, to the extent that you can grasp what their differences are. Your price might be posted for everyone to see, but how you communicate the *value* of your offering should reflect what you understand about each individual customer, one customer at a time.

Moreover, the value delivered in your customer experience will go up in direct proportion to the amount of friction you remove. Your offering will have more value whenever your customer spends less time and effort getting the product to work correctly, or re-inputting his settings or preferences, or checking whether he's getting the lowest price.

And because friction can also be costly to a company, removing it can provide compounding benefits. One of our clients, for instance, found this out in its own three-year effort to eliminate friction in its customer experience. By zeroing in on one source of friction at a time, this $20 billion telecom company was able to document not just a measurably better customer experience (more value for its customers), but it also eliminated nearly $2 billion in unnecessary process costs and generated an estimated $3 billion in added revenue.

In physics, friction is the inevitable heat waste generated by any closed system. In the physical universe this waste is always increasing, and the measure of the increase is entropy.

In business, friction is the extra effort that impedes a customer from efficiently meeting his or her need. But in the business universe, constant improvements in technology and the relentless pressure of competition mean that customer friction is inevitably on the decline. And the measure of this decline is value.

Avoiding Death by Procurement: Four Strategies

"There is hardly anything in the world that someone can't make a little worse and sell a little cheaper – and people who consider price alone are this man's lawful prey."

– John Ruskin (1819-1900)

I don't know about you, but at Peppers & Rogers Group I get very anxious whenever a customer sends us to the procurement department. Yes, procurement means we got the business (probably), but it also means we're about to take a big haircut on pricing and our profits are going to be put under the magnifying glass. As a consulting firm specializing in customer-facing issues, most of our clients are large, name-brand companies – companies with a great deal of buying power and negotiating leverage. Companies with powerful procurement departments that make me anxious.

I once interviewed a former executive at a big, well-known technology company to get his take on how his former company approached the vendors it bought from. What he told me: "[Our company] was always looked upon as the must-win account for every supplier, and we knew that well. So we routinely adopted very tough positions and made stringent demands."

According to this executive, when dealing with a smaller vendor his company would: "work closely with that company, study them, and try to extract as much of the process and knowledge as possible, then fire the supplier and do it ourselves. Overall, being self-sufficient was always a key objective. A few companies managed to avoid this ultimate fate by continually innovating faster than [our company] could absorb, so they maintained the ability to deliver new value each year."

Here are four strategies for avoiding the slow, painful death that a tough procurement department can subject you to:

1. **Innovate.** As the executive I quoted above suggested, to the extent you can stay ahead of your customer with innovative product or service

ideas, you'll always have something to sell. So your mission should center on being nimbler, more creative, and cost-efficient – all at the same time. The value you bring for the customer, however, is only partially found in the new product or idea itself. The reason the customer will want to keep dealing with you is because of your demonstrated ability to continue to innovate with even more new products and ideas. You have to keep the innovation wheels spinning fast without losing control of costs.

2. **Customize.** Any customized service or product configuration creates switching costs that increase a customer's willingness to continue buying from you rather than bidding out a contract at every opportunity. The trick is to ensure that whatever high-end services you develop can only be duplicated by your competitors with great effort, even if they are instructed in advance (and they will be – by your customer!). You want to make it more convenient for the customer to continue dealing with you, rather than going to the trouble of re-specifying with a competitor. So seek out the design engineers responsible for integrating your firm's components into the customer's final product, or the regional merchandising managers whose jobs depend on the programs you help organize for them. The richer the context of these relationships based on customization, the stronger they will be.

3. **Appeal to a customer's own end users.** A highly desirable brand name, or a product in heavy demand by your client's own customers, can be very effective at pulling your products through the customer's organization. The "Intel Inside" advertising campaign creates pull-through for Intel. When Mattel offers Toys-R-Us an exclusive arrangement for particular configurations, or for products with their own consumer brands such as "Barbie" or "Hot Wheels" or "Harry Potter," it is making itself indispensable to this very tough customer. Any service that saves time or effort for an end user will help, also. Dell's online services for enterprise customers, for example, not only save money for big customers, but also provide Dell with direct, one-to-one relationships with the executives who actually have the Dell computers on their desks (i.e., the end users).

4. Concentrate on finding "good" customers to begin with. Look for the kind of customer most likely to want to partner with suppliers, rather than exploit them. The best kinds of businesses to deal with as customers themselves will be the ones that that have strong internal cultures based on trust. Toyota might be considered such a customer. The five-part "Toyota Way" is a well-known set of values that have defined Toyota's business culture for years. It is a culture based on cultivating the trust of dealers, consumers, employees, and supply-chain partners, and the benefits have been significant for the company. Several years ago, for instance, when a sudden fire at one of Toyota's Tier One suppliers threatened to disrupt the company's production, several other suppliers proactively banded together and took the steps required to keep the assembly lines going, without even waiting to get formal approval from Toyota. They simply trusted that Toyota would do right by them, and the company did. So look for companies that already have long-term vendor relationships, which are a marker for true partnerships. Such relationships will be harder to dislodge, but once you gain a place at the table it will be worth every penny of sales effort you put into it.

CHAPTER 5

Deliver a Customer Experience That's Relevant to Each Customer

Reliability and value are important qualities of a frictionless customer experience, but every customer's own experience with a brand or product is personal and *unique to that individual customer*. The way one person perceives his or her customer experience is often different from the way others would perceive it.

Because of information technology, every business today has the ability to deal with these individual differences among customers. Moreover, because competitors have access to the same technology, every business *must* try to do so, simply to remain viable, and customers have come to expect them to. Customers are no longer satisfied by a customer experience that involves telling a company the same things about their wants and preferences over and over.

As a result, improving any individual customer's experience requires a business (1) to know something about that customer's uniqueness, and (2) to act appropriately on that knowledge. You must remember your customers, and you must use that memory to inform and perfect the actual experience you deliver to each of them. You must be *relevant*.

Don't Run Your Business on the Goldfish Principle

Certain species of tropical fish have no territorial memory. None. Perhaps this trait evolved because the species inhabited the open sea, where territory was not very important and territorial memory counted for nothing. But the fact is that no matter where such a fish swims today, it never recognizes the fact it has swum there before. We can imagine such a fish swimming around and around in an aquarium or a goldfish bowl and never getting bored, because there's always something new and interesting to see.

Many of today's businesses still operate on "The Goldfish Principle" when it comes to their customers. They evolved in the age of mass marketing, before computers made it possible to remember customers individually, so whatever business model they developed didn't rely on a customer memory. You can recognize a company operating on The Goldfish Principle when you sign up for a promotion with your airline or car rental firm, for instance, and then you still get a periodic email blast urging you to remember to sign up, or when you go online to your credit card website and schedule your payment a few days before the due date, but then they still send you an email reminder that your payment is almost due.

A colleague of mine tells a hilarious story of The Goldfish Principle in practice. On a business trip he was booked for three days at a nice hotel, and before going to bed the first evening he called the front desk to ask for a wake-up call. The cheerful desk clerk told him that as a premier business guest he was enti- tled to a "special offer." Would he like a complimentary coffee and newspaper brought to his room in the morning, five minutes after his wake-up call? My colleague said he preferred tea, if that was OK. No problem, said the clerk, and would he like the *New York Times* or the local city paper? Well, he asked, could he get the *Wall Street Journal*? Sure, she said.

In the morning everything went well, just as requested. The second night, my colleague again called the desk to arrange a wake-up call, and the clerk cheerily told him (again) that as a premier business guest he was entitled to a "special offer." Would he like a complimentary coffee and newspaper brought to his room in the morning, five minutes after his wake-up call? Yes but tea not coffee, please. No problem, came the reply, and would he like the *New York Times* or the local city paper? The third night it was the same story. So by the end of his stay, do you think the hotel had made this customer feel "special?"

With today's information technology there's absolutely no excuse for operating on The Goldfish Principle. It's actually worse than doing nothing, because it demonstrates a level of incompetence that destroys a customer's trust in the business. The hotel simply wanted to improve its customer experience, but it probably diminished it. And while it's convenient to be able to schedule a credit card payment a few days before it's due, if the company continues to remind you that the payment is due soon, you might find yourself having to check again whether the payment is actually scheduled or not. Just a few weeks ago I double-paid a credit card bill for this reason. And not long after that I found myself having to call my car rental company on the phone just to confirm that I was *already* enrolled in the promotion they had again emailed me about (I thought they might have emailed me because my first attempt to enroll had failed).

Operating on The Goldfish Principle today doesn't just communicate that you aren't competent enough to run a sound business, it screams that you don't care enough about your customers to even try to be competent.

Five Types of Customers by Their Value

At the vast majority of businesses, a minority of customers account for the majority of profits, whether they are split in an 80-20 manner or something less or more extreme.

And while we often speak of customers as having different values to a business, the truth is that the *value* of a customer is based on what that customer will buy in the future. What the customer has bought in the past is certainly one indication of likely future purchases, but past spending is already in the bank, and it's not the only information that would go into an estimate of future transactions.

There are really two separate ways to think about a customer's future transactions and purchases:

1. **Actual Value:** How much do we expect the customer to buy in the future, as of today?

2. **Growth Potential:** How much more *could* the customer buy, if we had the right marketing?

This reasoning leads to two "dimensions" of customer value that we can use to map customers into five different categories of value, as shown in the diagram below:

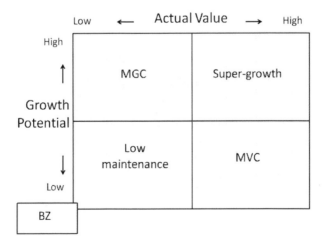

The way you treat these different types of customers will be based on their different "value profiles." Each value profile leads to different financial or business objectives, as follows:

- **MVC**: Each of your "Most Valuable Customers" (lower right quadrant) does a lot of business with your firm. They may not have a lot of growth potential, but they're each very valuable (they're part of the 20, not the 80), and your primary objective for these customers is to keep them. Customer retention tactics could include recognition programs, churn prevention analytics, and customization, among other things.

- **MGC**: Your "Most Growable Customers" (upper left quadrant) don't do much business now, but have a lot of growth potential, so your objective should be to actualize this potential. Tactics could include account penetration initiatives, product add-ons and value-adds, cross-selling, up-selling, and service enhancements.

- **Super-growth:** These customers (upper right quadrant) are more common in B2B situations. Typically, they are large enterprise accounts that already do a lot of business with your company but could do much more. Think Microsoft, or Google, or General Electric as customers. For these customers your objective should be to retain them *and* to grow their business. You might even have to re-think your business model to accommodate such growth.

- **Low-maintenance:** The vast majority of your customers probably fit into this fourth category (lower left quadrant). None of them is very valuable to you individually, but there are a whole lot of them. For these customers, your financial objective should be to improve your efficiency and streamline your operations. You want to reduce the cost to serve these customers, without reducing the quality of their customer experience. Tactics could include automated and self-service options, inside sales coverage, and mass customization.

- **BZ:** Finally, every business has a few "below zero" customers (very left side). These are the ones who cost more to serve than they're worth, and who have little if any growth potential. For some types of businesses

73

(retail banks, for instance), the *majority* of customers may actually consist of BZs. Your financial objective for BZ customers should be to re-architect your value proposition so as to (1) cover your costs, and/or (2) encourage defection (yes, I actually said that!). Tactics could include imposing fees on previously complimentary services (you can waive the fees for more profitable customers), or requiring a minimum amount of business to maintain an account.

The main reason you want to know how different customers compare in both their Actual Value and Growth Potential is to help you set different business objectives for each different type of customer. To realize those objectives, of course, you'll need to know more than their values. You'll need to know what each customer needs. And you'll have to launch different kinds of marketing campaigns, and make different kinds of offers, in order to appeal to each individual customer based, not on that customer's value to you, but on what that customer *needs* from you.

What Does It Mean to Be "Relevant" to a Customer?

British retailer John Lewis is trying to deliver a more relevant in-store customer experience by equipping sales personnel with tablet devices that can mimic the online experience. According to *Retail Week*[3], "Store staff will use the tablets to help shoppers decide what to buy, and their data trail will be collected in the same way as it is when shoppers buy online." And Fast Company[4] has reviewed the even more sophisticated technology that eBay is now testing for the fashion brand Rebecca Minkoff – again, in an effort to make the physical customer experience nearly as relevant and personalized as the online experience already is.

These examples illustrate how difficult it will be for brick-and-mortar firms to deliver an in-store customer experience that is truly relevant and individualized. But relevance will be critical for their long-term survival, so they work hard at it.

Other firms don't seem to work at it at all. Here's a copy of an email message that a colleague of mine received recently from Marriott Rewards, with a comically irrelevant message. It might as well broadcast "We don't care who you are but we really don't give a s**t anyway!"

For most businesses, the very best kind of customer experience is one that is frictionless, that is, reliable, valuable, relevant, and trustable.

But what does it mean when a customer experience is *relevant*? Well, if reliability is "product competence," then relevance can be thought of as "customer competence." To deliver a relevant customer experience, your company must be competent enough, in terms of processes, data, and systems, to treat different customers differently, and to treat each one appropriately for what you know about them, or what you *ought* to know.

The first requirement for delivering any kind of relevance, of course, is analytics. No matter what our business is, we all know that our customers are not identical. In my experience, however, business managers often don't appreciate just how different their customers are from one another.

At the most basic level of marketing, customers are different in terms of their value to a business. Some customers are clearly worth more than others, so most companies focus the majority of their customer-differentiation efforts simply on understanding different customers' different values – who are the most valuable customers, the most growable ones, the below-zero ones, and so forth. A customer's value profile allows you to set different financial objectives for different customers.

- In order to achieve your objective for any of these customers, however, you have to get that customer to behave differently in some way (i.e., to buy more, or to stay longer, etc.), and to do this, you must appeal to that individual customer's *needs*. But there's no single metric for customer needs. There are as many different categories and dimensions of customer needs as there are analysts trying to catalog them.

- The point is that being "customer competent" involves a lot more than simply tracking a customer's buying volume and frequency. It requires mixing the science of analytics with the art and wisdom of human judgment. So delivering a truly relevant experience to an individual customer is no walk in the park. Moreover, because the online customer experience can often be highly relevant, the contrast with a less relevant brick-and-mortar experience can be stark, which is one reason that forward-thinking retailers like John Lewis and eBay are trying to master the task.

- Clearly, being relevant to an individual customer is on the bleeding edge of delivering a more frictionless experience. But you don't necessarily have to be inventing new technologies. You can also become more relevant to your customers simply by applying existing technologies in a more customer-friendly way.

- In just the few days before writing this, for instance, I suffered through two different flights canceled by bad weather, on two different airlines. Both airlines texted messages to my mobile phone advising me of their flight cancellations. The first airline advised me of the cancellation and instructed me to call a toll-free number to rebook myself. The second one advised me of the cancellation and told me I had already been rebooked on a later flight, giving me the flight details and record locator number, and advising me that if I wasn't happy with the new flight I could either go online or call to change it.

- It should be obvious which cancellation notification was more *relevant* to me, and created a more frictionless experience.

relevant =
customer
competence

Four Technologies to Make the Contact Center Experience Relevant

We all know what it's like going onto some company's website to try to get something done, and not being able to figure it out, right? When we finally give up and call in, we can only talk to a human being after first doing battle with the robot voice, and then when we finally do get the rep on the line we have to explain things from the very beginning, because the rep has absolutely no clue what we just spent the last 15 or 30 minutes trying to do on the site.

In the United States, more than half of inbound customer service calls are now preceded by an online session of some kind. And since the vast majority of these inbound calls are in fact just as "disconnected" as I have described them, this means that whenever your contact center fields a live customer service phone call these days, there is a high probability that the customer is already upset and impatient.

So even though you may measure your contact center's performance in terms of its "first call resolution" rate, from the customer's standpoint more than half the time it's already their second attempt to solve the problem!

As bad as this disconnect is when it comes to customer care issues, it costs real money if you're talking about online sales. Imagine a prospect who searches your site for the right configuration, delivery schedule, pricing terms, or some other issue. The prospect can't find it and decides to call in, but this call is answered by a rep who has absolutely no insight at all into what the prospect was considering, how long she looked at certain options, what alternatives she considered, or anything else. So rather than routing your prospect's call to someone who specializes in the subject the customer was interested in, and rather than providing your rep with a click-stream record of the prospect's search so far, you have to start all over again.

Ironically, there are four simple, straightforward technologies available to eradicate this problem, but the vast majority of customer service contact centers don't use them, which is just one more reason why so many customers rate their call center experiences as sub-par.

1. **Click-to-call.** An increasing number of online searches take place on customers' smartphones, and it's easy for your website to recognize what kind of device a customer or prospect is browsing your site with. (Google even penalizes websites that don't offer mobile-friendly versions to mobile browsers, by reducing their ranking in mobile-based search results.) So when a customer is cruising your site from his phone, it makes sense for you to allow him to click a button to call directly from his phone into the contact center, all within the browsing experience itself. And of course, when this happens, the call's routing can reflect what the customer was doing on the site, and the answering rep can be shown the customer's click stream or other customer-specific data.

2. **Proactive chat.** If a customer isn't browsing from her smartphone, one of the easiest ways to give her some human-to-human assistance while she's on your website is to offer a chat window at the appropriate time. Be careful with this, because customers will simply tune out if they get a pop-up invitation to chat just by logging in. The right kind of chat invitation is one based on a tested algorithm that considers factors such as how long a visitor has already been on the site, what pages they've viewed, and how much time is spent on particular pages. Don't try to do it by the seat of your pants. Use analytics to set up your algorithm and test it until you get it right. But when you proactively offer to chat with a customer or prospect *at the right time* it's an ideal way to reduce abandoned shopping carts, buttress any low-performing pages on your site, or simply nail a difficult service problem with a minimum amount of hassle.

3. **The "Call Me" button.** If you're on Amazon's website and you can't get things figured out, rather than just calling the toll-free number, you can click the "Call Me" button, enter your phone number, and in a few seconds (or whenever you specify), someone from the contact center will call *you*. And hey, guess what? The rep who calls will already know

exactly what you were doing on the website when you clicked the button, and they'll also happen to be skilled in handling that particular issue.

4. **The temporal phone number.** Not many folks have heard of this, but it's an ideal mechanism for splitting the difference between proactive chat and "call me." When customers or prospects are on the client's website and decide to call in, they click the "contact us" button and what pops up is a toll-free number that is actually a unique, one-time-use phone number just for them. It will only be valid for a few hours, and when they call that number the call center's technology knows who they are and what web session they're connecting from, so their call can be routed to a rep who specializes in handling the products or issues they were just dealing with, and can see a record of the entire visit and click stream. (One client of ours saw a *ten-fold increase* in sales conversion using this process!)

These are all ways to do a better job of giving your customers or prospects a truly integrated experience, even when their interaction crosses over from online to contact center. If you want to reduce the friction in your customer's experience, you should already be relying on one or more of these mechanisms.

Are Your Biggest Customers Your Biggest Losers?

The CMO of a life insurance company once showed me a decile analysis illustrating which of his company's customers generated the most profit for his firm, and which ones generated the least.

A decile analysis simply arranges some quantity of financial information by decile – that is, by 10 percent increments. The insurance company's chart looked something like this, graphically showing the percentage of this company's profits over the last five years that were produced by the top 10 percent of customers, the second 10 percent, the third, and so forth:

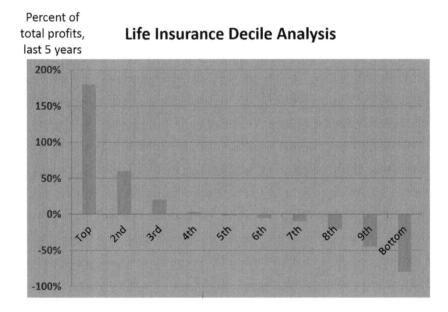

You can see from the bar chart that the top 20 percent of this company's customers actually accounted for *more than 200 percent* of all the profits earned by the company over the previous five-year period, while the bottom 60 percent constituted a net drag on profits. (You might be tempted to try to match this decile analysis to the 80-20 rule I wrote about previously, but be careful, because power-law distributions like the 80-20 rule are more difficult to fit to data that is both positive and negative, such as profits and losses.)

But this is just a side discussion. Now for the main event:

Let's overlay onto this graph a line that shows the "average face value" of the policies purchased by the customers in each of these different deciles:

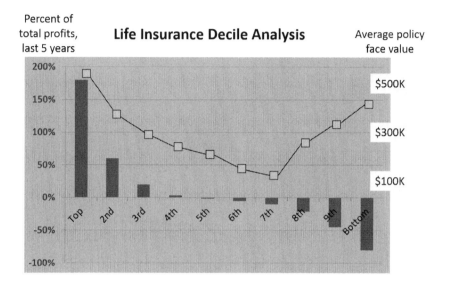

What the shape of this line clearly shows is that this company's most profitable customers *and* its least profitable, money-losing customers each tended to buy the highest-value, most expensive life insurance policies!

How can this be? Why would a high face-value policyholder be unprofitable at all? Why doesn't this line simply slope down and to the right, as policies become smaller and smaller, and therefore less and less profitable?

Before you suggest it, this profitability chart has absolutely nothing to do with actual death rates. It is an actuarially normalized chart, which means that whether a person dies and has his policy paid off has nothing to do with the profitability attributed to him, because the costs of death benefits are actuarially distributed across the entire customer base.

But if not death benefits, then what else could explain this U-shaped curve?

Actually, the answer is very simple, and it has to do with customer retention. As with many businesses, it costs money to acquire a new customer in the life insurance category. When a new policy is purchased, the company pays a sales commission. The typical commission amounts to more than two years' worth of profit on a policy. What this means is that, if a new policyholder terminates his or her relationship with the company less than two years after buying a policy, the company actually loses money on the customer. And of course, the bigger the policy, the more commission is lost.

It would be hard to come up with a more graphic depiction of the value of customer loyalty, right?

But I also like this graph because it clearly illustrates something else that is vitally important to marketers: A customer's acquisition cost is usually related to the volume of the customer's business, but not to the customer's *loyalty*. So while high-volume customers all cost more to acquire than low-volume customers, some of your biggest customers will also be your biggest losers.

The real issue for your business is how best to align your customer acquisition cost, not just with a customer's purchasing volume, but with customer loyalty, cost to serve, and other variables that contribute to a customer's overall "lifetime value."

Customer Loyalty: Is It a Behavior? Or an Attitude?

What does it mean when we say that customers are "loyal" to a brand? Does it mean they're a repeat purchaser? Or does it simply mean they *like* it? In other words, are we talking about physical actions, or does "loyalty" refer to a state of mind?

If loyalty is a state of mind, then being "loyal" to a brand or a company means that you prefer its products, services, or brands over others. In purely economic terms, you should be willing to pay a premium for your preferred brand, relative to others. Attitudinal loyalty is therefore closely akin to brand preference, customer satisfaction, Net Promoter Score, and other metrics designed to gauge the internal sentiments of customers.

Personally, I have a couple of problems with trying to define loyalty purely as an attitude. For one thing, attitudinal loyalty would be redundant with brand preference, so why introduce a separate term at all? Moreover, an attitude can be completely separate from any continuing relationship on the part of a customer, and this simply flies in the face of the common English definition of the word "loyalty." Customer A and Customer B might have an equally loyal *attitude* toward a particular product, but what if Customer A has never even consumed that product before, while Customer B has consumed it regularly in the past? In this situation, it wouldn't much matter whether Customer A was "willing" to pay a premium for the brand or not.

The behavioral definition of loyalty, on the other hand, relies on a customer's actual conduct, regardless of whatever attitudes or preferences underlie that conduct. By this definition, you should be considered a "loyal" customer because you continue to buy, period. It's not your mental state being measured, but your transactions, so your behavioral loyalty can be measured in dollars and cents.

However, the behavioral definition has its own drawbacks. It's quite possible for customers to *behave* loyally even when they don't really *like* a brand, provided there are other reasons for purchasing. An airline with poor customer service, for instance, might have customers who behave loyally but aren't happy about it, if it has the only nonstop flights between certain destinations, or even if its prices are significantly lower than those of other airlines. And some business-to-business firms selling complex services may rely on long-term legal contracts in order to ensure they are adequately compensated for high set-up costs.

Nor do you have to stretch your imagination very far to recognize similar situations. How do you feel about your bank, for instance? Many people hate their retail banks with a passion, but it's still just too much trouble to switch. Plus, they reason, the next bank's service will probably be just as lousy anyway. So defining loyalty in purely behavioral terms is just not very useful. In behavioral terms, monopolies have the most loyal customers of all.

For all these reasons, when you think about trying to improve your customers' loyalty, you need to pay attention to both definitions of the word simultaneously. Attitudinal loyalty without behavioral loyalty has no financial benefit, while behavioral loyalty without attitudinal loyalty is competitively unsustainable. What you want is a positive customer attitude that drives positive customer behavior.

So yes, you definitely need the NPS surveys or the CSAT surveys, but you must also correlate the attitudinal insights you gain with the actions you observe from these same customers.

If you don't keep both your customers' attitudes and their behaviors in mind simultaneously, then you'll be easily seduced into buying your customers' loyalty, rather than earning it. But while discounts, premiums, and reactive anti-churn policies can often be useful tactics, they won't contribute much to a long-term franchise as a business.

In the long term, you want to *do* business with customers who *want* to do business with you.

Improve Customer Loyalty by Recruiting Loyal Customers

One of the many inspiring stories told by Fred Reichheld in his classic book *The Loyalty Effect* has to do with Nissan's Infiniti brand and Toyota's Lexus. More than 20 years ago when they were launched in the U.S., each high-end brand was carefully engineered not just as an automobile of flawless quality, but also marketed as a customer experience unique to the automotive category – one designed to provide highly personalized, concierge-like customer service.

Yet despite their similar aspirations, these two brands developed very different patterns of customer loyalty. Early on, Lexus achieved a remarkable 63 percent repurchase rate among first-time buyers, while Infiniti only achieved a rate of 42 percent. While 42 percent was still far superior to the typical 12 percent to 30 percent car-brand repurchase rate in the United States, it was considerably less than Lexus, despite the fact that each brand had similarly sterling quality.

So what was the big differentiator? Why did Lexus customers show so much more loyalty than Infiniti customers?

According to Reichheld, it had to do primarily with the different types of new customers recruited by these two car companies in their initial marketing. Lexus went after Cadillac and Mercedes drivers – customers who tended to be older and attracted to comfort, long-term value, and reliability. But Infiniti positioned its brand to go after Jaguar and BMW drivers – customers more interested in style and performance. The customers Infiniti targeted, in other words, tended to be "experiential" customers who simply had a personal preference for new and novel experiences. An Infiniti owner, when seeking to purchase a new car, might say to himself, "Wow! That Infiniti was great! Now I want to try something else…"

The obvious lesson: If you want loyal customers, start by trying to recruit the kind of customers predisposed to be loyal in the first place.

 recommendation...

But this introduces another problem, because the kinds of customers who are personally more inclined to be loyal are going to be inherently more difficult and expensive to acquire in the first place.

Trying to solve this problem, Lexus found that one of its most effective recruiting tools consisted of recommendations from existing customers. But this was before Facebook, Twitter, and various online rating platforms made customer recommendations and word of mouth into the kind of marketing phenomena that they have become today.

Even before the e-social age, Lexus figured out a truly ingenious way to secure such personal recommendations, en masse.

Its secret? Well, in the ordinary course of business its dealers accumulated sales leads through advertising, promotional activities, and showroom visits. Dealers also had a growing database of existing customers, and feedback surveys revealed which of these customers were the most sincerely enthusiastic about their new cars, as well. So one of the most effective selling programs Lexus used was for dealers to stage an elegant, catered dinner or other event at the dealership, at which they would show off the vehicles. The dealer would invite sales prospects for this free dinner, promising that there would be absolutely no selling or arm-twisting at the event. In fact, the dealer would tell them, Lexus sales people would not even be invited to the dinner!

However, in addition to the sales prospects themselves, dealers would also invite current Lexus drivers whom they knew from their surveys to be particularly happy and enthusiastic about their cars. The seating was arranged in advance, so that each sales prospect was seated between two happy current Lexus drivers. It made for a great sales tool, with absolutely no selling required.

Best Buy → Amazon
TV

That Old-Time Customer Loyalty Feeling

We can easily define customer loyalty as a metric of success, but sometimes it makes more sense to think of it as a *feeling*.

At a business conference a few years ago, Jason Sadler, founder of iwearyourshirt.com and a highly creative marketer, related an anecdote about how Best Buy had helped him find the right flat-screen television. Apparently his living room had unusual lighting and dimensions, and he didn't really know what parameters were important, so he tweeted out an appeal. *Anyone know anything about flat-screen televisions?*

As he told the story, he soon received a reply from Best Buy asking him what the dimensions of his room were, and then where the light came from in the room—what side of the room were the windows on, and how big were they? After a number of such back-and-forth tweets, Best Buy recommended a particular type of television for him.

This, Sadler said, was amazing. He had been completely sold by a series of Twitter interactions. So he went to the Best Buy store and found the television that had been recommended to him. However, as he was in the store, prepared to buy, he decided to use his smartphone to search online for the same model, and guess what? He found it on Amazon for a lower price. What should he do? What would you have done?

Although his conscience pained him, Sadler said, he elected to save the money and bought the product from Amazon. But he tweeted back to the Best Buy folks to let them know, and their message back to him was something like "well, we're glad we could help. Maybe next time…"

Ever since, however, as Sadler related this story to the business conference, he said that he has looked for every excuse imaginable to patronize Best Buy. He goes to the Best Buy store for routine things, even when it's out of his way. He recommends Best Buy to friends who are in the market for electronics. And, he tells this story everywhere he goes.

So my question to you is, did Best Buy benefit or not from its interaction with Sadler? Was it stupid or smart for the company to spend time simply helping a customer find the right product to meet his need? The fact is, it lost the sale in the end, right?

Yes, and Best Buy lost it for the same reason many other brick-and-mortar retailers are losing sales to online companies—because the world is now completely transparent to customers armed with smartphones and connected 24/7. Why *shouldn't* a customer simply find the lowest price before buying a product? After all, in this kind of immediate buying situation, the products being compared are virtually identical. They are probably mass-produced by the same company at the same plant, so if one is even a dollar cheaper than the other, then that's a dollar in the customer's own pocket. (And Best Buy has since improved its online offering to ensure it is more competitive with other online merchants.)

But if this is your entire perspective, then you're missing a key point. Because in the process of giving Jason Sadler advice, just helping him to figure out what particular product would be right for him, Best Buy also created a bond. Even though the interactions were entirely via Twitter, Jason felt closer to Best Buy. He felt an obligation. It wasn't a legal or contractual obligation, but a social one. It was just a *feeling*.

Sadler felt he ought to repay Best Buy for the kindness it showed in helping him. He felt that he was in Best Buy's debt, and that he ought to give back, somehow.

My suggestion is that no matter what your business is, this is the feeling you want your customers to have about you. If your customers have a genuine affection for you, if they simply *want* you to succeed as a business, then ultimately it's more likely you will.

Maybe genuine customer loyalty isn't measured just in dollars and cents, but in feelings and emotions.

Feedback

CHAPTER 6

Seek Out Customer Feedback

You'll never get an accurate picture of how customers experience your product or service if you don't listen to what they say. Hearing feedback from customers is essential if you plan to improve the customer experience over time.

But hey, guess what? Customer complaints come unsolicited, and they're a great source of feedback all by themselves. They don't require a survey mechanism, or a research firm, or tabulation software. They're free! So, studying customer complaints is a great "first order" method for gaining insight into the customer's perspective, and to identify the kinds of friction you need to eliminate in order to deliver a better customer experience.

#EpicFail: Are You Hearing Enough Complaints?

One summer day a boy we'll call "Jimmy" entered a small town's hardware store and asked the proprietor, a successful local entrepreneur, if he could borrow the phone. "Sure," the man said. The entrepreneur couldn't help but overhear the boy's end of the conversation, which basically went like this: "Hello, Mrs. Wilson? My friend and I cut lawns for money all around town and I just wondered if you'd ever like us to cut yours?... So, someone already cuts your lawn? Well, are you happy with the job they're doing? Sure we couldn't take a crack at it ourselves?... OK, then, well, that's good that you have someone you can depend on, thanks for your time anyway."

With that, Jimmy put the phone down and headed back out of the store, but the entrepreneur felt sorry for him and wanted to coach him a bit. "Jimmy," he said, "you have wonderful, engaging style, and that was a really nice sales pitch just now. Very professional. But selling is a numbers game, Jimmy. I've built more than one business in my time, and one thing I know is you have to try again and again. If you called 10 people just like her, I bet you'd be cutting two or three more lawns this very afternoon!"

The boy smiled somewhat shyly, and replied, "Actually, sir, I wasn't trying to sell Mrs. Wilson anything. The truth is, you see, my friend and I already cut her lawn. I just wanted to be sure she's happy with what we're doing." Then he excused himself, turned, and left to tend his business.

Question: Who is the smarter entrepreneur?

Jimmy was practicing something called "complaint discovery." When it comes to delivering a good customer experience, complaints and dissatisfaction are the single biggest indicator of areas that can be improved. And customer loyalty isn't as highly correlated with customer satisfaction as customer *dis*loyalty is with customer *dis*satisfaction.

Rather than trying to surprise and delight customers with ever-increasing acts of heroic service, in other words, you might generate better financial results for your business if you just took care to find and redress problems, fix things that go wrong, and directly confront the complaints that customers encounter.

But what if a customer never voices her complaint to you? What if she only tells her friends, or family members, or work colleagues—or her Twitter followers? The average complainer tells nine or more others about an unhappy experience. So successfully resolving a complaint is not only likely to generate increased business from the complainer, but also to restore nine or more potentially lost opportunities with other customers or prospects. The point is, if you're not hearing any complaints this might be a reason to worry, rather than to congratulate yourself.

To maximize your own business success, and to keep your customers as loyal as possible, you need to ensure that you are able to address more and more complaints. It might sound perverse, but the more complaints you discover, the more opportunities you have to build your business. A few things you can do:

- **Make it easy to complain.** Be sure to publicize both a toll-free number and an email address for customer complaints or comments of any kind, in addition to making it a simple option on your website. Give customers multiple avenues for voicing any problems. And monitor these channels 24/7. Outsource the function if you have to, but don't simply "close your ears" because it costs money to listen!

- **Monitor social media traffic for any mention of your brand, your product, or your business, and reach out immediately to complainers.** Twitter has become the complaining channel of choice for many today, so don't let those complaints go untended. It's better to respond within minutes, rather than hours. Letting more than a few hours go by is unacceptable.

- **Follow up after a complaint is resolved.** Make sure the customer is happy with the outcome. After handling any unusual or stressful transaction, be sure to ask the customer for permission to follow up in a few days. And during such follow-ups, don't try to sell anything with this outreach. Just verify whether everything went OK, and ask how your company might have done anything better.

Customer Experience Is a High-Wire Act, Customer Service Is the Net

In their excellent book *The Effortless Experience,* the Corporate Executive Board's Matthew Dixon, Nick Toman and Rick DeLisi write that a positive product experience generates word-of-mouth more than twice as often as a negative one. However, when it comes to a customer service experience, just the opposite applies: a negative service experience gets shared with others twice as much as a positive one.

Take a look at the two graphs below, from their book:

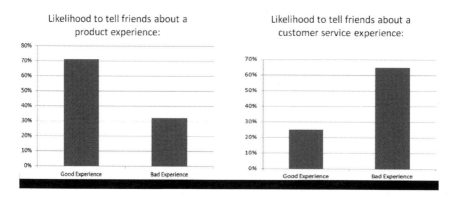

We can speculate about why this is. Perhaps people find it more personally satisfying to tell others about a product they just bought because a great new iPhone or a new car with terrific features, or even a really practical household device reflects well on the purchaser's expertise. But, a customer service experience often occurs via the corporate contact center, after the product experience isn't up to snuff. No one rushes to tell their friends about how great a company's phone service was. Instead, stories of "customer service hell" are simply entertaining to tell, in a "you won't believe this" kind of way.

In that spirit, a colleague of mine recently emailed me his own very entertaining "you won't believe this" tale of woe at the hands of an airline's reservations and customer service call center, which I have condensed here:

My wife and I have just had several days of poor customer experience with [XXX airline], trying to upgrade our daughter's seat on a flight to Indy to be closer to her friends up front. It would cost $67 …or I was going to try to use miles.

First we tried to complete the upgrade online, but were told we had to call the 800 number to do an upgrade with miles. So over the weekend we called in several times and went through the IVR each time. It takes several minutes to go through the IVR to get to "Awards Travel" because you first have to attest to all this info about non-hazardous materials, etc. And each time, when you finally get to awards travel they don't have an option that's relevant, so you have to ask for a representative. Three times they said: "Due to storms on the East Coast, we are experiencing an extraordinarily high volume of calls. Please call back later."

When I finally reached someone they said, "Sorry, I can't help with Awards travel, let me transfer you." Then they transferred me to a queue where I waited for 90 minutes more, before finally hanging up to go to dinner. Three days later, and after multiple attempts we still haven't been able to speak with anyone about upgrading with miles, despite the fact that this is what their own website said we had to do – speak with someone.

The next day my friend sent me an update:

OK, we have a resolution to this story, and you won't believe this.

My wife called back for a fifth time and got to the awards travel queue where she was put on hold. Twenty minutes later a man picked up and asked if she'd been helped and she told him what she wanted to do. He said "I can't help you with that" and put her back on hold.

Another 40 minutes later, she finally spoke with someone who could help with rewards upgrades. She wanted to upgrade a coach seat to a premium seat near the front using rewards *points, rather than have to pay the $67 fee. She was told that they only allow points to be used to upgrade to first class. My wife said she just wanted to upgrade to the premium seat and was told they couldn't do that.*

So, my wife said, "I've been on hold with your company for four hours over the last several days and you're telling me you can't help me with this?" and then pleaded, "Is there anything you can do since it's been such a difficult experience?" She was told there was nothing they could do if she didn't want to use points to upgrade to first class.

…so that's the resolution – four hours of effort after seeing instructions online to call for help with points upgrades. And in the end they told us they can't help her use points to upgrade to a premium seat.

There are plenty of opportunities to screw up your customer service process, and the bigger the screw-up, the more entertaining the story will be, as it's passed around among your customers. I find it highly ironic that whenever a company treats the task of handling customer interactions as simply a necessary cost of doing business, all the effort that goes in to minimizing that cost will actually have the reverse effect.

This story is compelling not because anyone should dictate how an airline allows its own customers to use mileage points to upgrade to Premium Economy. It's entirely within every company's individual discretion to decide its own pricing and product configurations.

The point is, *whatever* a company's policy is, it should make it easy for customers to get their questions answered online, on its automated website. Either that, or it needs to make doubly certain that a customer can get an explanation via the call center, and without hours of pointless effort – bad weather or not. Problems like this can provide hours of entertainment for other customers.

If delivering a good customer experience were a high-wire act, then customer service would be the net. And when the net fails, even a slight flaw in the experience will be fatal, no matter how lofty a company's intentions are.

Tapping Into the Hidden Value of Complainers

If you put one pot of boiling water and another pot of lukewarm water into your freezer at the same time, guess what happens? The boiling water will freeze first! This phenomenon has been known since the time of Aristotle, but apparently even today no one understands precisely why it happens. Recently, in fact, the U.K.'s Royal Society of Chemistry put up a £1,000 prize for the first person who can offer a satisfactory explanation.

Similar to freezing a pot of boiling water, companies can often turn the most vociferous of complainers into raving fans—brand advocates who are even more convinced in their positive views than other, more satisfied customers are. And, this is a phenomenon that isn't so hard to explain.

While rapid technological progress and rising levels of interactivity are clearly raising customer expectations in general, a complainer is someone whose expectations are, shall we say, downwardly mobile. If you feel a company has wronged you in some way, then you'll examine every new interaction for evidence to confirm this personal belief. (This is your confirmation bias at work. Don't even bother trying to deny its existence.) As a result, something that might have begun as a flawed company policy of some kind, or an oversight or simple mistake by someone in the firm, could soon be interpreted by the complainer as bad intentions on the company's part. And bad intentions constitute the most serious breach of trust possible.

Trust is largely a social concept. The trust a customer has in your company reflects not just the customer's own independent opinion, but also how the customer's friends evaluate you. Even a single complainer's dissatisfaction and distrust can soon infect a large number of others. So complainers, if left to their own devices, can do immense damage to the overall value of your customer franchise.

However, the mere fact that a complainer has already developed a particular point of view means that as soon as the company does something to contradict that point of view—reaching out to handle the complaint proactively, for instance, or apologizing sincerely and trying to make things right—its action has the potential to completely reverse the customer's mindset, violating the customer's expectations once again, but this time in a positive manner. The more a business contradicts the customer's own pessimistic expectations, the more noticeable and memorable its initiative will be. When done right, like the boiling pot of water that freezes faster, a simmering complainer will often become a highly convinced brand advocate even faster than someone who never had a complaint to begin with.

You probably already know this to be true, simply from personal experience. But what it means for your company is that a complaint, once it is voiced to you, is an opportunity to improve your bottom line. So when your company is fortunate enough to hear a complaint from a customer, your policies and employee training should support five simple actions:

1. **Acknowledge:** Always begin by acknowledging the complaint and the complainer. Whether or not you think a complaint has merit, you have to start by granting the legitimacy of the complainer's point of view. Empathy is a very powerful cure-all, but it must be displayed freely and without reservation on your part.

2. **Apologize:** There's no substitute for simply saying "we're sorry." No ifs, ands, or buts—just plain old "sorry for this." As the complainer tells you what's wrong from his or her perspective, apologize early and often. With feeling.

3. **Amplify:** Probe for any additional information about the complaint. As the complainer vents to you, and as you are acknowledging the complainer's problem and apologizing for the inconvenience or for whatever other injury the customer incurred, keep asking if there is anything more—any further dissatisfaction that has not yet been voiced. Get it all out.

4. **Ask:** Once the problem has been fully exposed—when the complainer says there isn't anything more—you should ask the single most important question: What does the customer think would be a fair and satisfactory resolution? How can your company remedy the injury?

5. **Act:** Then, if it's at all possible, do what the customer has just told you would be fair. Or go even further, if you want to see that pot of boiling water cool faster.

Changing the Definition of "Integrated Marketing"

For years, one of the most common buzzwords in the sales, marketing, and customer service disciplines has been "integrated marketing."

Originally coined in the late 1980s, this term has traditionally stood for the kind of marketing and sales promotions that are closely coordinated across all media. Basically, you want your marketing to be "integrated" so that it doesn't look like it came from different companies, and its various offers and appeals don't overlap or conflict with each other.

Wikipedia's current article on "Integrated Marketing Communications" tracks at least three successive definitions of the concept over more than 25 years:

- From the American Association of Advertising Agencies in 1989: "an approach to achieving the objectives of a marketing campaign through a well-coordinated use of different promotional methods that are intended to reinforce each other."

- From Northwestern University's Journal of Integrated Marketing in the 1990s: "a strategic marketing process specifically designed to ensure that all messaging and communication strategies are unified across all channels and are centered around the customer."

- From Brian Bennett's Stirology blog post[5] in 2013: «the development of marketing strategies and creative campaigns that weave together multiple marketing disciplines (paid advertising, public relations, promotion, owned assets, and social media) that are selected and then executed to suit the particular goals of the brand."

Excuse me, but all these definitions (even Bennett's, unfortunately) seem so...20th century. Today, integrated marketing must involve not just integrating your own messages and communications, but integrating your *customer* more directly into the actual marketing, sales, and service processes.

Technology is smashing all these functions together like never before. Marketing, sales, and customer service are smearing into each other with each new channel opportunity and smartphone app. The only *truly* integrated view of the entire start-to-finish process is the customer's own view.

So I would propose a slightly different, and simpler, definition for "integrated marketing" today:

> **Integrated marketing incorporates an individual customer's own perspective into all the customer-facing functions at a company, including marketing, sales, and service.**

Truly integrated marketing, in other words, happens when a specific, individual customer's own worldview infuses all the customer-facing processes that affect that customer. Truly integrated marketing would be if:

- Your Web marketing campaign generated a lead, and instead of tossing that lead over the fence to the sales organization to be pursued like every other Web-generated lead, it was instead packaged into a customer-specific selling strategy based on the expressed preferences and other insights already learned about the customer.

- Your customer's smartphone app automatically displayed his flight's boarding gate and on-time status as he entered the airport, because the phone already knows where he is and has access to the flight information already on his calendar.

- A customer called your company on the help line, and along with the service issue being satisfactorily resolved, a cross-selling opportunity relevant to the customer's own needs was also pursued, either in the same call or in a subsequent message.

I don't know about you, but I'm ready for some TRULY integrated marketing. I've about had it up to here with marketers thinking that all they need to do is just get their own act together.

You want to leapfrog your competitors? Try integrating the customer into your marketing, sales, and service activities, one specific customer at a time.

Is Your Customer Survey Really Useful?

Voice-of-customer ("VOC") feedback is always useful, but it's not always used correctly.

Not long ago I attended a presentation by a senior executive who was charged with collecting voice-of-customer feedback from the business customers served by his very large technology company. He based much of his presentation on some figures that were compiled from more than 100,000 online customer surveys completed over a year's period.

His VOC feedback program yielded some very helpful insights, particularly in the form of the many verbatim comments collected. Also, it allowed the company to identify and reach out to those who expressed high levels of dissatisfaction. So far, so good.

But then the executive told us that his company was so committed to improving its overall customer experience that senior executives at the firm all had a portion of their incentive pay based on the survey's results. That's too bad, I thought, because the way this particular survey was structured meant that it was virtually worthless in terms of understanding the overall level of customer satisfaction.

This was because his VOC survey was based on a highly biased sample. Good for anecdotal feedback and identifying specific problems, but nearly useless for understanding the general level of customer satisfaction within the entire customer base.

Here's why: All customers were solicited for their inputs virtually every time they completed any kind of transaction on the company's website, and there were nearly 4 million such transactions during the year. So 100,000 survey completions, in fact, amounted to a response rate of less than 3 percent. The problem is, with that low of a response rate it's almost certainly the case that those who chose to go to the trouble of completing the survey did so because they were either highly displeased or highly pleased with their interactions.

Remember, these were business customers. They were busy managers and IT executives who don't have a lot of spare time to begin with and aren't likely to dedicate even a few minutes of it to helping some other company figure out how to do its job better. Unless, of course, they were extremely unhappy, and wanted to give the company a piece of their mind, or perhaps extremely pleased, and eager to share their good wishes.

Using such data to infer overall satisfaction levels would be like sticking one hand in ice water and the other in scalding water, then inferring that, on average, you must be quite comfortable.

It doesn't matter how large your VOC sample is, if your sample is biased it will be far less useful than a smaller but less biased sample. Rather than soliciting everyone and netting a 3 percent response (even if that amounts to 100,000 or more respondents), you would do better by soliciting just a couple of thousand participants chosen at random, and offering them some form of compensation or benefit designed to generate a higher participation rate. There will still be some bias in the results, but far less than in a universal survey that suffers from an extremely low participation rate.

With just a few tests you might even be able to find some combination of prizes or fees that would generate an 80 percent or 90 percent participation, which would give you much greater assurance that the busy executives whose opinions you were now collecting more fairly represent the entire population you are trying to serve.

The only truly unbiased voice-of-customer feedback, however, is the feedback you find entirely "in the wild" – simply by observing the comments made by your customers to their friends and colleagues, mostly in social media.

Non-Invasive Voice-of-Customer Feedback

The "observer effect" is one of the strangest principles of quantum mechanics. The act of observing something in the quantum realm determines whether the something you are observing is a wave or a particle. Before an actual observation, it is either or both, but once it is observed, it will only be one or the other.

Similar to the observer effect, obtaining VOC feedback is not as easy as surveying your customers to ask their opinions, because the act of asking the customer will contaminate your results. Not that surveys don't produce useful data, but genuine voice-of-customer feedback is subject to its own "observer effect," over and above any biases introduced by insufficient sample size or survey techniques.

When I ran marketing for a small airline, one of the things I did was to record a random 30 minutes of inbound calls at our reservations center. Basically, I would choose an agent and time of day at random, then record his or her calls for 30 minutes at that time. With this done, I made several copies of the recording and distributed it to the half-dozen or so other senior executives at the airline, so each of us could listen to it on our way to work the next day. This constituted our voice-of-customer program, a bit rough-hewn but at least free of any observer effect. .

Resourceful executives go to great lengths to obtain uncontaminated – that is, truly unbiased – voice-of-customer feedback. Chip Bell and John Patterson, in their marvelous book *Wired and Dangerous*, tell us that the mayor of Santa Clarita, California meets regularly with hairdressers in the town, because they are likely to have the real scoop on what citizens have been saying. And the manager of a hotel in Texas schedules focus group meetings with taxi drivers, because he knows that his hotel guests are more likely to share their honest opinions with them than with the front desk manager or in an online survey.

Fast-forward to the e-social era, and VOC feedback can increasingly be obtained "in the wild," that is, on a variety of interactive and social media platforms where customers make their opinions known without having to be asked for them. Gathering VOC feedback in a non-invasive manner is likely to become an extremely common activity in the future.

Satmetrix now has SparkScore, for instance, a social media analysis tool that can help a client deduce a company's implied Net Promoter Score without surveying its customers directly. It does this by examining the strength and pervasiveness of positive and negative sentiments, on a variety of social media platforms, from Twitter and LinkedIn to specialized customer forums and communities. (Obviously, one of the capabilities this offers is to assess a competitor's NPS numbers as well.)

And non-invasive voice-of-customer feedback can also be used for discovering business-building opportunities on a one-to-one basis with individual customers. For one of our financial services clients, for instance, the audio files of inbound calls were digitally analyzed to identify any mentions of a set of important life events (births, retirements, college plans, etc.). It turned out that more than 2 percent of inbound calls had potential "selling opportunities" related to such events, and analysis showed that if just 10 percent of these opportunities could be closed, the client could realize a total increase in customer lifetime values of more than $200 million.

Big Data has arrived, and Big Data means that the era of non-invasive voice-of-customer feedback is upon us.

CHAPTER 7

Personalize the Customer Experience

Every customer is unique, so every customer experience is personal.

An essential capability required for any business to be able to ratchet up the quality of its customer experience is the ability to personalize how it approaches each one.

Treating all customers the same is how the vast majority of businesses have operated for the last 150 years or so – basically ever since mass production processes took over the modern economy. It's only the arrival of computer technology that allows enterprise-sized businesses to track individual customers, discern their differences, and then try to accommodate each customer's own individual preferences and needs.

Knowing how your customers vary from one another is important, but that's only half the battle. The other half is using technology to render different services, offers, and even individualized products for these different customers, in order to deliver *humanity* to them, at scale.

Loyalize Customers by Remembering Their Needs

When I'm on a business trip I'm a sucker for a quiet evening in my hotel room with a room-service pizza. One time, while staying at a Ritz-Carlton hotel, I called downstairs for a pizza, then resumed working on my laptop until the knock on the door came about 30 minutes later. Only then did I realize I'd forgotten to request red pepper flakes. I *love* red pepper flakes on a pizza. How do people even eat pizzas without red pepper flakes?

In any case, I opened the door and the waiter wheeled in the room-service table with my pizza, a soda, some utensils, and….a small dish of red pepper flakes! Hooray, I thought. At least *this* hotel knows how to serve a pizza!

I signed the bill, but as the waiter was just about to leave, I had a thought. I asked him whether they served red pepper flakes with all their pizzas. "No," he said, glancing down quickly to check his pad, "but *you* like them, don't you?"

I had completely forgotten that this was not my first room-service pizza at a Ritz-Carlton, and they had already noted my preferences. From my perspective, it just seemed like Ritz-Carlton had the best pizza.

Customized products and services are important tools for any company trying to improve its customer experience. Treating different customers differently is the very essence of what makes a customer experience relevant.

When customers tell you how they want to be treated, and then you *do* treat them that way, you are providing them with a kind of service they simply can't get anywhere else at any price – at least not without first re-teaching someone else what they already spent time and energy teaching you.

This is one of the primary reasons why people engage with the same e-commerce site over and over again, whether it's NewEgg, Amazon, eBay, or someone else – because once you've already given the site your credit card information and shipping address, it's so much easier just to keep going with them. Provided, of course, that they don't screw up, and that some other site's prices aren't significantly lower. I say "significantly" because most people aren't going to give up all the convenience of shopping somewhere that already knows them unless the price difference is significant enough to make up for the effort. It might vary with the customer, but convenience saves time, and time is money. Different people will attach different values to it, but at some level everyone wants convenience.

So if you want to loyalize a customer, try remembering some specific need or preference the customer has communicated to you in some way, and deliver on that need without having to be reminded.

Dealing with Customer Variability

There is a famous scene in the 1970 movie *Five Easy Pieces* in which a young and surly Jack Nicholson is stymied in his effort to get a side order of plain wheat toast at a roadside diner. Told by the waitress that the diner doesn't serve plain toast (it's not on the menu), he asks her whether he can get a chicken sandwich on wheat toast. When she says yes, Jack says OK then, bring "a chicken sandwich on wheat toast – no mayonnaise, no butter, no lettuce," and then adds "and now hold the chicken."

Fast forward to the present. A woman goes into a Starbucks and asks for a simple glass of milk. Real milk, 2 percent please, *just* milk. According to her account,[6] this not-so-routine request of a Starbucks barista almost caused his head to explode. "Mocha," he called out, but she had to correct him. Twice. And even though she asked for just a glass of milk, the first time it arrived it had been steamed, so it had to be re-ordered. (Cold, please. Ready to drink. M-I-L-K.)

Starbucks, like the roadside diner and any other business, tries to maintain its quality and control its costs by standardizing processes and operations. Routine tasks, if they can't be automated, are at least handled in the same way by every employee.

But customers are all different. They want different things – different sizes of products, different delivery dates, different specifications for services, and so forth.

On one hand, customer variability like this creates an opportunity to generate loyalty, because by remembering individual customers and their preferences, we can create relationships that are durable and long-lasting. This can generate better profits for you provided you minimize costs by using computer power to automate the process.

But on the other hand, not all customer variability is so easy to deal with, and if you don't have a routine process for automating how you handle it then your production and service delivery operations can suffer. According to Frances Frei and Anne Morriss, in their very useful book *Uncommon Service: How to Win by Putting Customers at the Core of Your Business*, a few of the different forms that customer variability can take, in addition to specific requests and preferences, include:

- **Arrival times**: Grocery stores, for instance, are often crowded during the evening rush hour, while the lines at Starbucks can be interminable just before the workday begins.

- **Capabilities**: Some customers need more hand-holding than others, which means the cost of serving different customers can be quite different. For instance, whether a patient can accurately describe her own symptoms or not has a big impact on how costly it is to provide adequate medical care.

- **Effort**: Some corporate controllers are well organized, while others are not, which changes the economics for an auditing firm handling the account. Some shoppers return their shopping carts to the store, others don't.

Variability like this is something Frei and Morriss call "customer chaos," and they suggest it can be managed in two basic ways: either by eliminating it, or by accommodating it. If you choose to eliminate variability, you will generate more efficiency. If you choose to accommodate it, you will generate better service.

And whenever you launch a new product or begin selling to a new market you have to be prepared for an increase in customer variability. This is one of the things that makes it so difficult to accommodate multiple business models under the same corporate umbrella.

When Dell Computer began selling enterprise-level servers, the authors say, "the company knew the corporate market for these machines would create significant new service demands, which it would have to accommodate with around-the-clock assistance. Dell faced a choice between destroying its margins by creating an underutilized and expensive service infrastructure or falling behind competitors that had more efficient operations. Dell landed on a creative solution—outsourcing service to a third-party provider optimized for these kinds of 24-hour, on-site service calls. By doing so, Dell reduced its exposure to customer variability by essentially handing off the challenge to a company better prepared to manage the challenge."

Handling customer variability is never going to be a walk in the park. Under some circumstances you might be able to turn it into a competitive advantage, but you also have to be prepared either to minimize it, or to lay the risk off to a third party, as Dell did.

And perhaps next time our Starbucks customer, who just wanted a glass of milk, would get a better result if she were to ask for "a tall skinny latte, no steam. Now hold the coffee."

Customized Pricing? How to Do It Trustably

A few years ago I was listening to incoming phone calls at a call center run by a Peppers & Rogers Group client. This was a credit card and financial services firm, and for about an hour I sat directly behind one of its best agents with an extra earphone to my ear, listening to her incoming calls and conversations.

As I listened, a caller said she had just received an offer for a competitor's card with a reduced fee of just $25 a year and a very low interest rate, so she was thinking of switching. The agent tapped a few keys and replied, "Well yes, Mrs. Smith, actually we have that same card available. In fact, my records show we sent you an offer for a card with these terms back in April. The offer was included in your billing statement, but maybe you didn't see it. If you'd like this card now, why don't I just send it out to you? We can even give you a retroactive credit for three months' worth of the higher annual fee you've been paying..." Naturally, the customer was delighted.

About 20 minutes later, after handling several other calls, the agent received virtually the same inquiry. A man said he'd received an offer for a $25 card at the same low interest rate (from the same competitor), so he was thinking of switching. However, after tapping a few keys this time, the agent replied, "I'm sorry Mr. Jones, but we just can't match that offer at this time. We do hope you'll choose to stay with us, though. Is there anything else I could help you with?"

We all know what was going on in these two calls, right? Mrs. Smith was obviously a good customer, probably more creditworthy and more profitable for the credit card company than Mr. Jones. This is an example of what economists call "price discrimination," and it is a perfectly legal and highly useful economic practice. Unlike racial or ethnic discrimination, there is nothing illegal or unethical about offering a product at different prices to different customers (as long as you aren't basing your offer on race or ethnicity, of course). Airlines and hotels set different prices based on different travel restrictions, B2B companies negotiate different prices for different clients, movie theaters have special deals for children and senior citizens, and Florida theme parks give discounts to Florida residents. These are all examples of price discrimination.

By charging different prices to different customers a company is simply trying to maximize the profit obtained from *each* customer. After all, customers are all different. Some will desire a product more than others do. Some will be more likely to buy on impulse, some will buy more often, some will trade quality for price, and some will be more particular about getting exactly the right brand.

As common as it is, however, price discrimination can easily be perceived as sneaky and untrustable. A recent *Wall Street Journal* article described a massive survey involving tens of thousands of online shopping events that revealed websites engaged in very sophisticated forms of price discrimination, sometimes charging different customers different prices based on how far each customer was from a competitor's store, physically. And while no one would think it odd for a brick-and-mortar store to compete more aggressively with stores in its own neighborhood, somehow the idea of having different prices quoted to us by an e-commerce company operating over the Web seems manipulative.

Of course, being technologically manipulated by a vendor is only offensive if you actually find out about it, and for now at least, most people don't. But what technology giveth a business today, technology can taketh away from the business tomorrow. And it won't be long now before social filtering tools allow consumers to find out for themselves the lowest price a company is currently charging for a product or service among all its customers, or even how to take advantage of a company's pricing algorithm itself. In the case of one supermarket chain's program, for instance, the *New York Times*[7] interviewed one shopper who, "[L]ike any good shopper...is already starting to game the system: she noticed that she received cheaper prices on ground coffee when she alternated between Starbucks and Dunkin' Donuts brands rather than buying just Starbucks."

Some online aggregator sites are already experimenting with services that will make a kind of "reverse scalping" possible – meaning that consumers will be able to make their own personalized discounts available to other consumers, either for a fee or just for the satisfaction of it. And with smartphones, customers will gain access to this kind of information and make this kind of decision even while they're in the store.

Customer trust, however, will be harmed whenever customers feel they've been taken advantage of, or that they were simply fooled into paying more than they needed to. If, for instance, slight product modifications come to be seen as a mere smokescreen for charging customers as much as they are willing to pay, or if the complexity of the pricing system itself is overly complex or confusing to a customer (as is the case with airline fares and mobile phone plans, for instance), then a business is on thinner ice, and the trust customers have in a firm can be damaged.

So, if you operate a business with scientifically individualized services and pricing, tailored to the different situations of different customers, what should be your strategy?

My advice: Treating different customers differently is not untrustable, per se, but trying to conceal what you are doing from customers is. In the case of the call center where I listened in on calls, I suggested to the client that it should prepare in advance for the possibility that sooner or later two customers getting different offers might compare notes, because they are neighbors, or good friends, or work at the same office. So if and when Mr. Jones calls in to ask why he didn't get the same offer that Mrs. Smith did, the company needs to be able to explain exactly what he can do if he wants to receive it – raise his credit score, go six months without a late payment, spend more per month, something like that. (And, of course it would have to do this without violating Mrs. Smith's privacy.)

If you want to improve profits with individualized pricing while minimizing the risk of erosion of trust, I suggest:

1. Position your program externally, and think of it internally, as a way to offer tailored discounts, rather than as a way to extract higher prices;

2. Assume your customers, individually, will find out how your individualized discounting decisions are being made;

3. Have a policy for "negotiating" with individual customers for different discounting terms, based on clear criteria; and

4. Above all, in any dispute, problem, or policy decision, strive to be "fair" with each customer – simply treat the customer the way *you* would want to be treated if you were that customer.

Improve the Experience by Not Giving Customers Choices

Yes, I know it sounds absurd, particularly from a one-to-one marketing "guru," but not giving customers choices will often improve the customer experience. Let me start with a story from my own life.

A few days after our family moved into a new house, my wife took me furniture shopping. We needed a new sofa, she said, to match some of the other new stuff we had acquired for our expanded living room. As we neared the furniture super store, I saw a billboard atop it proclaiming "Thousands of Sofas to Choose From!" and my heart just sank. This was going to be just AWFUL!

As contrary as it might seem, you are not doing your customer any favor by offering thousands of choices, or even dozens. The act of choosing is an imposition. It's friction, plain and simple, because you're asking customers to do your work for you. Yes, the customer will want something just right, and yes, every customer may want something different. But the choosing of it is still an onerous activity.

It is a well-known principle[8] in the direct marketing business that one of the surest ways to *reduce* the response rate in any communication with a customer is to require the customer to make a choice. Want fewer people to respond to your offer? Be sure to ask whether they prefer Option A or Option B. Want a further reduction in response? Offer Option C. Requiring a customer to make any choice at all is, by itself, an extra burden of effort. More often than not, in a direct marketing campaign this effort alone will overwhelm whatever likelihood you had of getting a response.

This doesn't mean that choice is always wrong, but you have to approach it carefully. One wise use of customer choice is for gathering insight on a particular customer – learning the customer's actual preferences. An automotive company I once worked with launched a loyalty program and offered new members their choice of gift for joining: a pair of racing gloves with the brand's logo on them (it was a kind of sporty car), or a package of three children's videos, or a collapsible umbrella and road atlas. In this case, making the choice was extremely simple, didn't involve a decision about how much money to spend, but simply what free gift to accept. And the option chosen revealed a great deal to the auto company with respect to how to treat each different customer in future interactions.

Another wise use of choice is when it serves as a mechanism to stimulate customer thinking, or to give them ideas. Not all customers really know what they're searching for. They may prefer to meander a bit, trying to zero in on something. But the fact that a particular customer likes to meander is itself a bit of customer insight you should also tuck away. Different customers view the shopping experience differently.

If you have a wide variety of sizes, specifications, prices, colors, delivery options, and the like, then one way to reduce the burden of choosing is to mass-customize. Don't eliminate the choosing process altogether, but reduce it by using categories. Modules.

Imagine, for instance, that the furniture super-store my wife and I visited had made this offer to us, online: "Pick the price range, base colors, and preferred styles you will be shopping for and before you come to the store we'll propose a selection of no more than 10 'most-likely' choices to start your search…" Or better yet, what if they had said "Send us a picture of the furniture you're trying to match and we'll have a small selection picked out for you."

You really want more sales? Try to reduce the number of choices customers have to make in order to get what they want. Requiring customers to choose is friction. Eliminate it.

Use Interactions to Maximize Customer Insight

In the heyday of the dot-com boom, one online pet supplies retailer asked a single, fact-based, yes-or-no question of its website visitors, designed to identify those with the highest potential for spending on their pets. This is an example of what we call a "Golden Question" – a customer interaction specifically designed to reveal a great deal of insight about customers, but without subjecting them to a battery of marketing research.

If it is designed well, a Golden Question can often generate highly useful insight without even appearing to be a survey or a marketing inquiry at all, and it can often be fun or interesting for the customer to answer. Like the automotive company from the previous essay that offered new loyalty club members their choice of gift, a Golden Question is simply any customer interaction designed specifically to elicit important and useful insight.

One of our former consulting clients, for example, was a vacation time-share company. Research had shown that vacation time-share customers used their membership in two different ways:

- "Vacationers" tended to buy a time-share at a particular resort they liked, and then they would vacation there regularly, allowing the company to rent their property out in the meantime to defray the ownership cost.

- "Traders," on the other hand, liked to exchange their time-share property for other owners' properties at a variety of different resorts, and they would usually vacation at different times and places each year.

For obvious reasons, the company wanted to be able to tailor its offer and sales pitch appropriately in order to address the different needs of these very different types of prospective customers. But how could it decide, as soon as the discussion started, which category any particular prospect belonged to?

It turned out that the most useful and predictive characteristic of a trading family was that they had no young children at home. So during any discussion with prospective new customers, the sales rep would ask about children. If the family included young children, then it was almost a certainty they would not be trading their property much, at least not until the children grew older.

And in the world of Big Data, Golden Questions are easier than ever to find. OkCupid, the matchmaking website, has analyzed thousands of different questions asked to millions of customers, and it turns out that the single question that does a better job of predicting relationship longevity than any other is: "Do you like horror films?" (Go figure.)

As these examples all demonstrate, it isn't always necessary to administer a 50-question survey or subject a customer to detailed scrutiny in order to gain insights useful enough to provide a more relevant customer experience. Figuring out the right Golden Question may generate just the insight you need. And it can be fun, too.

As for the pet supplies retailer? Its Golden Question was: "Last year, did you give your pet a holiday present?"

Mass-Customizing the Customer Experience

The first task in treating different customers differently is to recognize and remember how they are different, both in terms of their value to you, and in terms of what they need from you.

But the next task is to render different "treatments" for different customers. In order to scale this process economically you have to reduce the need for manual intervention or constant human oversight. The automated process for rendering different customer treatments is called "mass customization."

No matter what kind of customer experience you're trying to mass customize, you need to think carefully about two different tasks in order to do it proficiently:

1. How the customer *specifies* his or her preferences or requirements, and

2. How you *remember* them and apply them.

The first task, the specification process, represents a kind of "design interface." In a make-to-order world, your business needs a convenient but accurate way for a customer to specify exactly what kind of customer experience he or she needs. That is, they need to be able to design their own treatment. If your design interface involves strolling around a three-acre warehouse to find the right sofa, or waiting eight weeks for the made-to-order product, not only is it inconvenient for the customer, it's also costly for the business. Better to offer the customer a series of simple choices (but not too many) in order to capture the primary differences among your customers. Do you prefer warm colors or cool? Home delivery or pick-up? Monthly invoicing or quarterly? Postal letters, email, or text messaging?

And the second task, remembering, involves your customer database or CRM system. You can only make it irresistibly convenient for a customer to continue doing business if you actually *remember* what each customer has specified, individually. So train your sales and service people, and anyone else entering data into your CRM system, to listen carefully for each customer's individual preferences or desires, and to be meticulous about recording them.

Both these aspects of customization – specification and memory – must be correctly mastered in order to turn the act of customization itself into an effective competitive tool for getting, keeping, and growing customers.

Now think about how you can break down your production and service delivery process into different components, or "modules," each of which can be combined with other modules in order to deliver a specific, relevant customer experience. By pre-configuring just a few modules to be combined into different offerings, you may be able to render thousands, or even billions, of possible customer experiences.

To keep the customer's experience as frictionless as possible, start with whatever customer insights you already have, and then walk the customer through as few additional choices as necessary to arrive at the correct offering for that individual.

In addition to a product's physical attributes (size, color, etc.), there are *many* aspects of the overall customer experience that could be tailored to an individual customer's need. For instance:

- **Configuration**: Without changing the physical product itself, perhaps you could pre-configure a system to your client's needs. Acumen Vitamins, for instance, are offered in pre-configured daily assortments, often including a dozen pills or more, based on a health questionnaire and an analysis of a single strand of the customer's hair.

- **Packaging**: How many variations of packaging make sense for different types of consumers or business customers? Would seniors want smaller, lighter packages with instructions in larger type? Would professionals like different or more detailed product information? Which customers would prefer multi-packs, or perhaps mini-packs?

- **Ancillary services**: Should the equipment come with regular maintenance or calibration service? Should the new car come with quarterly detailing, monthly wash-and-wax, or automatic pickup and delivery when it's time for maintenance? Should the warranty for your device or product be tailored to the customer's own intended use, perhaps in terms of copies-per-month, hours-per-day, or miles-per-quarter?

- **Additional products**: What additional products contribute to meeting a particular type of customer's need? This might involve accessories (story books with LEGO sets, insurance with automobiles, cages with hamsters, or sweat socks with sneakers). It could involve replenishable supplies (oil changes for automobiles, pet food for hamsters). Or consider offering high-volume customers a greater quantity than everyone else gets – a dozen bars of soap, five dozen golf balls, or a half container-load of product instead of a single pallet.

- **Pre-authorizations**: Some B2B companies help their customers enforce preset authorizations to fit different corporate approval systems. Vice presidents are allowed to order leather desk sets and unlimited paper supplies, for instance, while secretaries are pre-authorized for routine purchases up to $200 per month.

- **Invoicing and payment terms**: Are invoices sent at the convenience of the customer or at your own convenience? Are they developed in the most desirable format for a customer, or for ease of issuance by your accounting department? When you notify a customer by email that his bill is now available online, do you provide any other helpful information in the email (like total due, or due date), or do you make the customer log in to find this out? Do you anticipate cash discounts? Some buyers prefer smaller payments and longer terms, while others seek to forestall payment and are happy to pay the price.

CHAPTER 8

Earn Your Customers' Trust

From the beginning of commerce, customer trust has always been important to a business.

Most authorities on the subject have talked about customer trust in terms of two different qualities – good intentions and competence. Do you, as a business, have good intentions towards me, your customer? Are you going to act in my interests? And are you competent to do that? Both of these qualities have to be positive for me to trust you. It does me no good if you have the best of intentions but your product is poor quality, cannot be delivered on time, or breaks when I use it.

As the rush of technology empowers us to interact more and more with others, trust has become ever more important, not just to businesses, but to *everyone*. We don't have time to stop and count our change at the cash register every time. We expect businesses to act in our interest, in general – or at least not to be sneaky and take advantage of us when we aren't watching.

What Does it Mean to be "Trustable?"

The fourth component of a truly frictionless customer experience – after reliability, value, and relevance – is trustability. "Trustability" is a precise word, designed to capture the nature of customers' increasing demands. And it may just be the most important frictionless component of all.

Whenever two people interact—either face to face or online—one of the most important subtexts of that interaction is trust. Trust greatly improves the efficiency of any person-to-person interaction, so as technology increases the speed and volume of interactions, trust becomes more and more important. If you don't trust someone on the other end of an interaction, it slows you down. It's a hassle. A pain. You have to check your facts, and count your change. You might even have to get your own lawyer or auditor involved.

In addition to this, interactions themselves generate transparency, so the increasing efficiency with which we all interact makes it ever more difficult to keep secrets. Whether we're talking about WikiLeaks or the latest customer service snafu at a pizza restaurant, the world is more obviously transparent than it ever has been.

Teenagers will tell you it's much harder to cheat on their boyfriends or girlfriends than it was before everyone was on Facebook. It's much harder to cheat on your customers, too.

So customers are starting to hold the businesses they deal with to a higher standard. They want "*proactive* trustworthiness,» and the term I use for this is "trustability." It's no longer sufficient for a business simply to do what it says it's going to do and charge what it says it's going to charge. That would certainly be trustworthy—it's not cheating or lying—but it's not *trustable*.

A trustable company will remind customers if a refund is due, warn them in advance before a warranty expires, or even advise them if it looks like they're buying more than they really need. Being trustable means protecting the customer from careless mistakes, poor judgment calls, lack of knowledge, oversights, and other self-inflicted problems.

The easiest way to explain trustability is to provide a quick example from the way Amazon delivers its customer experience. I buy a lot of books (as well as other things) from Amazon, and the Amazon experience is quite frictionless already. I might be reading some article online, and if I see a book referenced that I ought to get, I simply bop over to Amazon, find the book, click on it, and it comes directly to my house or my Kindle, because Amazon already has my credit card and address information. Easy peasy.

One day I read an article that referenced a book I thought I should read, so I went to Amazon and clicked on it. But this time, instead of getting confirmation that the book would be immediately delivered, I received a message: "Warning: You already bought this book from Amazon. Are you sure you want to buy it again?"

No, I didn't need two copies of the book. I'd just forgotten about previously buying it.

Of course, had Amazon simply gone ahead and shipped me the book it wouldn't have been cheating. It wouldn't have been dishonest in the least. But it wouldn't have been trustable.

And here's the thing about trustability: My experience dealing with Amazon is now even *more* frictionless, because not only do I not have to provide my credit card and address information, I don't even have to check my bookshelves first, to see if I've already got the book. If I already have it, Amazon will tell me.

Trustability takes friction out of every customer experience, and because interactions are coming so fast and furious now, this is even more important than it used to be.

Your customers already want trustability, today. Tomorrow, they'll demand it.

The Rapidly Evolving Trustability Opportunity

On a family vacation once at a South African game preserve, we were out in a safari vehicle and spotted a pair of rhinos grazing in the distance. Parking the vehicle, our guide suggested we get a closer look by approaching on foot quietly from downwind, so the rhinos wouldn't smell us. But the rhinos wouldn't see us, either, because they were facing away from us, into the wind. Puzzled, I asked our guide why a grazing animal wouldn't naturally have learned to face downwind rather than upwind. For millions of years predators have sneaked up on their prey from downwind, just like we were now doing. He told me that they graze upwind because the grass tastes better that way. The more tannin a grassy plant has in its leaves, the more bitter it will taste. And large ruminants emit flatulence that can be detected by many grasses, triggering them to draw more tannin into their leaves whenever grazing animals are about. As incredible as it sounds, therefore, grass-eating animals graze into the wind so the grass doesn't know they're coming.

Evolution is a truly beautiful mechanism for ensuring that life persists and prospers. And with all due respect to any reader's religious beliefs, God could hardly have chosen a more intelligent way to design life than by employing the inexorable, yet beautifully intricate, dance of evolutionary forces.

But evolution can also serve as a metaphor for how an economy actually operates. Creativity and innovation propel virtually all economic activity, as the best innovations prosper and replicate themselves, while less desirable innovations go extinct. Companies innovate and adapt to others' innovations in order to attract more customers and outdo their competitors, while consumers evolve too, as their own expectations and preferences change. Every innovation, therefore, poses both a challenge and an opportunity to an existing business. Adapt to the competitive threat, or harness it and use it to threaten your own competitors.

And the rising tide of trustability represents exactly that kind of innovation – one that will either threaten a business or become an asset to it.

This was driven home to me by an incident with my cable provider not too long ago. My wife and I got home one evening to find our cable service on the fritz. And our *favorite* series reruns from *Law & Order* were on USA that night, too! When I called my cable operator to find out what the trouble was, I got an automated message that there had been a disruption in our area, but that the company was working on the problem and hoping to restore full service by late that evening. OK, I thought. Stuff happens.

And sure enough, the next morning the problem had been remedied. But after more than 20 years of thinking and writing about customer experience issues, I've become a particularly demanding customer myself. So I called the cable company again. Call me cheap, but I wanted to be sure that my monthly bill showed a credit for the day we had to go without cable. It wasn't so much the amount involved (tiny), but the principle.

When I spoke to a rep he confirmed that yes, my account would indeed be credited, no problem. Then I asked him whether they had already planned to give me this credit, because since the problem was clearly something that had affected my whole area, they knew which households were in fact due for a refund.

His answer: "No, we only give refunds to the ones who call and request them."

This is, of course, a perfect example of the difference between trust and trustability. It's not untrustworthy of the provider to wait until a customer claims a refund to issue it, but the *trustable* thing would be to proactively advise customers that because an outage lasted for some particular amount of time, a credit will be automatically applied to the bill. No call necessary on your part, because we know you experienced this outage, and we're watching out for you.

And just think how customers would react! How would *you* react if your cable or phone company sent you a message saying "Sorry! We'll keep trying to do better, but in the meantime we're taking $1.27 off your bill this month because of last night's outage, and thank you for your continued loyalty?"

In isolation, it may sound like a costly initiative for any cable provider to refund even a few dollars to thousands of customers at a time, but the point is that sooner or later this policy is *inevitable*. Whether or not my own provider initiates it, sooner or later one or more of its competitors will, and then it will be forced to follow suit anyway.

When the natural environment changes, all organic species must either adapt to that change or perish. And when the business environment changes, all business species must adapt, as well.

Trustability Is the New Black

Most businesses today would consider themselves trustworthy, and by 20th century standards they definitely are. They post their prices accurately, they try to maintain the quality and reliability of their products, they refrain from cheating or stealing from customers, and they generally do what they say they're going to do. But for the 24/7 connected consumer of the 21st century, this kind of trust is no longer enough.

Consumers today demand *proactive* trustworthiness, or trustability. They want companies to help them manage their own best interests.

But even today, lots of businesses still generate substantial profits by fooling customers, or by taking advantage of customer mistakes or lack of knowledge, or simply by not telling customers what they need to know to make more informed decisions. Whole business categories are based on tricking customers out of their money. Yes, I'm perfectly serious. Think about it:

- For credit card companies, a marginally sophisticated borrower who can never resist spending, rolls his balance from month to month, and often incurs late fees is considered a most valuable customer! At some credit card companies, in fact, the term used to describe a credit card customer who dutifully pays his bill in full every month and never incurs a late fee is "deadbeat."

- Mobile phone carriers regularly and joyfully profit from contract customers who enlist for more expensive plans than their voice and data usage actually requires, or from roaming and data services accessed by accident. Just a few years ago, for instance, one major mobile carrier was caught instructing its call center reps not to voluntarily tell customers how to disable the buttons on their phones that often resulted in erroneous and expensive data charges[9].

- Retail banks in the United States make a substantial portion of their operating profit from overdraft charges and other fees assessed for what are usually just simple customer errors. One of the principal reasons banks began encouraging customers to use debit cards a few years ago, in fact, was that debit card usage tended to increase the number of inadvertent overdraft charges[10].

- The poster child for untrustability, however, is probably AOL, which has made billions by fooling customers into paying more than they need to pay for the services they get, and by making it ridiculously difficult for a customer to stop subscribing. A colleague of mine told me she took a job there as a customer data analyst in the late 1990s. She said AOL did A/B testing on everything: all their policies, promotions, marketing, and service initiatives. It discovered through testing that the most cost-efficient way to reduce churn was to hide the "cancel my subscription" button on the website, and to require people to call in before being able to cancel. It even began to intentionally disconnect inbound phone calls prematurely whenever the caller first mentioned their desire to cancel, in order to require a second call.

All of these business practices and others like them are destined to become extinct, and probably within just the next decade or so. Companies that engage in these kinds of untrustable practices will soon be out-competed by new entrant businesses that do a better job of ensuring a more frictionless customer experience – an experience based on proactively watching out for customers' interests.

The practice of making money by fooling customers or taking advantage of them is on the way to becoming entirely unfashionable.

Trustability is the new black.

Gross Incompetence Implies Bad Intentions

To earn a customer's trust, the customer must think you have:

1. Good intentions; and

2. Competence.

But while good intentions and competence might sound completely unrelated, the fact is they are joined at the hip.

Recently a colleague related an experience he had had with a major airline. This airline is highly regarded for its good service. As a consultant he's a very frequent flyer and he told me he had been nearly the first one to board one of its recent flights. As he took his seat in First Class (a perk for all who travel!), the flight attendant took his jacket and hung it for him, and he sat down and soon became engrossed in some work on his laptop.

Unfortunately, however, at some point prior to takeoff another flight attendant mistakenly thought that his jacket must have belonged to one of the previous passengers on the flight that had just arrived (because the aircraft had just emptied and no other jackets were hung yet). So unbeknownst to my colleague or the first flight attendant, she immediately rushed the jacket out to the gate agent where a page could be issued for the passenger who had left his jacket on Flight XX to please come back and retrieve it from the gate.

It wasn't until after landing at the destination that this mistake was discovered, at which point the flight attendants were both extremely upset (as was my colleague). They frantically called the previous airport to try to ensure that he could connect with his jacket. But no luck.

He said he applauded the flight attendant's initial motives, which were simply to be sure all customers were given above-and-beyond service (going to great lengths to return a passenger's forgotten jacket), but he added that he was very disappointed with how the airline itself handled his problem from that point on. No one at the departure airport would even let him (or the flight attendants) talk to anyone at the gate where he had boarded the plane. Instead they told him to call "Lost and Found." But, he said, after calling for more than two days, no one from Lost and Found had ever answered the phone or returned his messages.

While this airline's flight attendants obviously had good intentions, and had been trained to try to protect the customer's interest at all times, apparently the company itself was totally incompetent when it came to helping this customer resolve an unanticipated problem.

The reason good intentions and competence go hand in hand is because if you don't put enough effort and investment into your processes and systems so that you can be reasonably competent when it comes to managing your customer's experience, then how good can your intentions actually be?

As it happens, two other colleagues of mine recently related similar stories about their dealings with two other companies, both highly respected customer-centric brands. One colleague told me she had recently had a very bad customer experience with a home-improvement store. The evening after this experience she received a call from the store's parent company asking her how her experience had been. So she took the opportunity to complain, telling the company that she had been highly dissatisfied, thought she had been mistreated, and so forth. After that, she said, nothing. Nada. It never contacted her again. No call, no email, no letter, nothing.

Her verdict: They must be bad people. She can no longer *trust* them because they obviously don't care for their customers at all.

Another colleague emailed me recently to complain about an overnight delivery service, because in his opinion it had become completely unreliable, and had lost its customer-oriented focus. From his email:

> *They are awful now with splitting up ground and express…one can't pick up packages for the other, and it's hard to get in touch with ground to schedule them to pick something up,* etc.

> *I think they are on their way down based on how their changes are hurting customer experiences, I will never use them again if I don't have to.*

His verdict: He can't trust the company anymore.

My verdict on each of these companies, the airline, the home-improvement chain, and the package delivery service: Their intentions are good, but they are incompetent. Their systems and technologies just don't connect well enough to be able to carry through on what they want to do, which is to deliver a good customer experience.

On the surface, these are good companies. They make all the right noises about serving the customer's best interest. But in the end, if they don't care *enough* about respecting their customers' best interests to invest the time and money required to fix their various dysfunctional systems and processes, then how good can their "good intentions" actual be?

The lesson in all this: Don't think that by cutting back on your investment in technology and systems you won't undermine your reputation with customers. If you aren't competent, your customers still won't trust you.

Five Requirements for Being Trustable

Trustability is a word that Martha Rogers and I "re-appropriated" in our book *Extreme Trust: Honesty as a Competitive Advantage.* I say we re-appropriated it because the word "trustable," while rarely used, is already defined in the dictionary as a synonym for "trustworthy." Martha and I were looking for a single word, a *new* word, to encompass this new standard of proactive trustworthiness that consumers are increasingly expecting, so we re-appropriated "trustability" to serve that purpose.

There are many aspects to being trustable, but if you had to summarize it, you could talk about five overall requirements:

3. Demonstrate **Humanity**. To be trustable, a business must act toward its customers the way one human being would act toward another. Humans have *empathy,* and humans are *fallible.* To have empathy a business has to see things from the customer's perspective, demonstrating genuinely good intentions toward them. As for fallibility, just think about it: Your business is already fallible. Every business is. All you have to do to demonstrate humanity to your customers is admit to it once in a while.

4. Be **Competent**. You have to be both product competent and customer competent. Not only do you have to have a product and service quality at least on a par with your immediate competitors, but you have to be able to treat different customers differently and maintain individual customer relationships that grow stronger with every interaction.

5. Think **Long term**. You can't be trustable if you're entirely focused on the short term. Customers are the link between short-term actions and long-term value for a company. If you don't have the ability to embrace the long term, then don't even think about trying to become more trustable. Eventually your flawed arithmetic and off-center metrics will do you in.

6. **Share**. People enjoy sharing things with others. If you want to be trustable your business has to share, also. Share your ideas, your technology, and your data. Make your intellectual property more freely available, in order to stimulate innovation. Trust others the way you want them to trust you. And remember: You can only harness the power of social production with trust, not money.

7. Respect **Evidence**. Don't manage by judgment alone, but rely on evidence. Evaluate information for its objectivity and accuracy. And take the steps required to deal with the inevitability of random events: Pay more attention to numbers and statistical best practices, measure inputs in addition to results, and plan more carefully for alternatives and multiple scenarios.

CHAPTER 9

Let Your Humanity Shine Through

If your plan is to improve the customer experience you deliver, then at some point you have to acknowledge that on the other end of that experience is an actual thinking, breathing human being – a *customer*. And while all of us humans are certainly capable of complex reasoning, calculation, and planning, our thinking processes and our very beings are still dominated by the very emotional quality of *being human*.

As humans, we experience joy and happiness, sadness, regret, anxiety, nostalgia, jealousy, pride, and the whole rainbow of other emotions. We want to connect with others, to belong, to be appreciated, and to be loved.

Our strongest motivations are usually not rational thoughts, but emotional feelings, and scientists who study how people think are increasingly of the opinion that it is our *emotions* that more often drive our decisions, which we "explain to ourselves" with our rational thoughts.

Never overlook the human element in a customer experience.

Frictionless First, Then Delightful

For the vast majority of businesses, the ideal customer experience is not so much delightful or surprising as it is frictionless. It's an experience that requires no extra time or effort and imposes the least possible burden on the customer.

This is because unless you first do a good job of meeting the customer's need and solving his or her problem, then "surprise and delight" won't be very compelling. In fact, if your product or service isn't frictionless to begin with, trying to "wow" a customer might even call attention to your failures.

However, after you've made your customer experience reliable, valuable, relevant, and trustable – the four primary qualities of a frictionless experience, then delighting or wowing a customer with something unexpected, or something "over the top," can in fact be a very effective way to gain that customer's genuine emotional commitment to your brand.

Delivering an over-the-top, delightful experience doesn't necessarily require a heavy expense. It may, in fact, involve no expense at all. The most direct way to connect with a customer emotionally is simply to allow your own humanity to show through.

After all, smiles and empathy are free.

Even small bicycle parts don't cost too much. At Zane's Cycles, a Connecticut bicycle "super store" doing some $13 million of business, if you come in to acquire a part for your bike, and the part costs less than a dollar, they don't charge you for it. And if you think about the rationale it makes perfect sense. As Jeanne Bliss relates in her classic customer service book *I Love You More Than My Dog*, if all you're coming in for is a tiny part, and you only need one of them, then you've already spent more time and energy than this part would be worth just by getting into your car and driving to Zane's.

But being empathetic and kind to customers isn't limited to small businesses or retail merchants, either. The massive and hugely successful UCLA Health System has a reputation for delighting its "customers," i.e., the patients it serves. That's right, you can become terribly ill, go through a series of traumatic procedures, be subjected to painful treatments, and yet leave the institution utterly delighted – not just because you were cured, but because you were treated in an extremely human, and humane, manner.

The UCLA Health System's entire culture is based on reaching out to patients individually, showing respect and courtesy, listening to their problems, and responding to their issues. It's not just the quality of the medical care that makes this institution successful, but the quality of *care* – the quality of its attention to the human beings who are its patients. Similar stories could be told of other fine medical institutions, such as Mayo, or Cleveland Clinic, or Geisinger.

And at Southwest Airlines, the flight attendants are well known for their playful shenanigans, often hamming it up in front of customers, not to mention going the extra mile to ensure that everyone enjoys the flight, even when it's crowded.

Importantly, each of these businesses is competently operated and has already eliminated all possible points of friction in its customer experience. Southwest runs a tight ship, more on-time and dependable than most airlines. And it wouldn't do Zane's a bit of good to give away bike parts if the bicycles it sold weren't up to par, nor would it matter how nice the service was at the UCLA Health System if patients still found themselves buried in forms, or having to explain their symptoms over and over again to different physicians or nurses.

But another important quality that each of these organizations has in common is a unifying corporate culture and sense of mission. It is this sense of mission that unites individual employees around a common purpose, which is to act in the interest of the customer. A culture like this ensures that all customer-facing workers are empowered to be empathetic and caring, spontaneous, creative, and even playful – in short, *human*. And the human quality of this kind of service is what delights a customer.

Because it offers a glimpse into the humanity within an organization, true, customer-oriented service can create a genuine emotional bond. In turn, the customer is likely to begin thinking of the company more as a friend, rather than simply as a faceless seller of goods and services, to be compared with all the other sellers.

So yes, first eliminate all the friction in your customer experience. Wring it out. Make things operate like clockwork for the customer's benefit and convenience.

But then, once you've done that, seal the deal by letting your humanity shine through.

Make Your Customer Laugh Once in a While

With all the serious talk about listening and responding to customers, monitoring social media, innovating, cutting costs, recovering from mistakes, etc., the very idea of being customer centric can begin to sound like really hard work.

But, maybe it doesn't always have to be. Maybe you should occasionally just have some fun with your customers. Make them laugh.

My brother Jeff is an Army chaplain. An ex-Ranger, he has no hair on his head and looks like the kind of body builder you wouldn't want to tangle with. Apparently one of his dietary secrets is the zero-calorie noodles he orders online from Miracle Noodle. The other day, after placing an order online, he received this email notification:

> Dear Mr. Peppers:
>
> Your noodles (order 221579) have been gently taken from our highly secured warehouse with cotton gloves and placed onto a satin pillow.
>
> Our team of employees inspected your Miracle Noodles and polished the labels to make sure they were in the best possible condition before mailing.
>
> Our packing specialist from Japan lit a candle and a hush fell over the crowd as he put your Miracle Noodles into the finest box that money can buy.
>
> We all had a wonderful celebration afterwards and the whole party marched down the street to the post office where the entire town of Chatsworth waved 'Bon Voyage!' to your package, on its way to you, in our private Miracle Noodle jet on this day, (5/6/2013 2:43:00 PM).

I hope you had a wonderful time shopping at Miracle Noodle. We sure did. Your picture is on our wall as "Customer of the Year". We're all exhausted but can't wait for you to come back to Miracle Noodle.

Shipped Via Carrier Priority Mail, Medium Flat Rate Box

Shipping Tracking Number 9405510200986079715532

Warm Regards,

The Miracle Noodle Team

I'm sorry, but I found this send-up of the standard customer-service message that "your product has shipped" absolutely hilarious!

At the end of its email, Miracle Noodle included an acknowledgment that the idea was "inspired by Derek Sivers." Sivers was the founder of CD Baby, an online music store launched in 1997 (before iTunes) that specialized in music by independent artists. Sivers also represents a great source for original ideas about how to do business, most of which can easily be accessed at http://sivers.org. And it's quite obvious that he likes to have fun.

Maybe we should all have a little fun with our customers once in a while!

Earning your customers' trust requires you to "demonstrate humanity." You want your customers to think of your business not as a big, bureaucratic organization with rules and procedures and lines of software code defining how things are done, but as a human organization, full of warm-blooded human beings with all the emotions and qualities of other humans - like customers themselves.

So yes, part of being "human" is to acknowledge mistakes and vulnerability, but part of it also is to have fun, to play, and occasionally to be silly.

Try it sometime. Your customers will like it, and they'll like you.

Delight Customers With Your Humanity

Nearly all descriptions of the quality of the customer experience have two basic components to them.

- The first requirement for providing a good customer experience is to eliminate problems and obstacles, making it as easy and painless as possible for the customer to meet her need or solve her problem.

- The second requirement is to please customers – to delight them with something enjoyable, or surprise them with something unexpected.

There is a priority to these two customer experience tasks. Don't even bother trying to accomplish the second task (providing enjoyment), if you haven't fully accomplished the first task (eliminating friction).

Forrester's Harley Manning and Kerry Bodine suggest a "Customer Experience Pyramid" in their recent book *Outside In: The Power of Putting Customers at the Center of Your Business:*

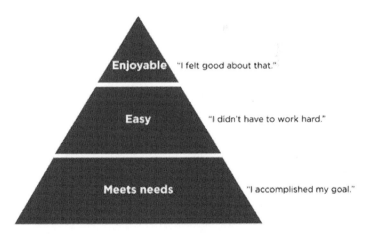

Although Manning and Bodine's pyramid involves three levels, it's easy to simplify their argument to the two basic components I described above, because meeting the customer's basic need and making it easy are both about removing friction. Only after you do these things, Manning and Bodine say, can you benefit substantially by making the experience enjoyable.

Assuming you first eliminate the friction, however, "enjoyment" is not just some attribute or function in the customer experience. Enjoyment is a human *feeling*. An emotion. A sense of pleasure. And while it may be linguistically correct to say that a customer can "enjoy" a perfectly functioning product or service (i.e., a customer experience that is frictionless), this isn't really what we're talking about.

An enjoyable – or delightful – customer experience involves *pleasure*, not just satisfaction.

And where does pleasure come from? It comes from some kind of emotional connection within the experience itself. It comes from your *humanity*, as a business.

You can convey humanity to a customer in a number of different ways – as many different ways, in fact, as there are emotions and feelings in the human mind. But here are a few ways to think about it:

- A customer could easily enjoy an experience when you make it entertaining in some way. For some companies, the value proposition itself is based on some aspect of entertainment – at an amusement park or club, a fine restaurant, or luxury hotel, for instance. But even commodity products can enliven and "humanize" their customer experience by injecting some entertainment value in it, perhaps with a hilariously tongue-in-cheek confirmation email message, such as the one my brother received from Miracle Noodle (see the previous essay).

- A simple thank-you note or hand-written communication can also make a human connection, provided that it's personalized and relevant to the customer, and not just something written the same way to every customer. When you check in to a hotel these days, it isn't unusual for there to be a hand-written note in your room from the hotel manager, hoping you have a nice stay. However, while it's certainly a valiant effort to make a connection with a customer, in most cases these notes are not personalized at all, beyond the name of the guest, perhaps. How much more delightful would it be for me to find a note from the manager that said "on your last visit, you bought some Diet Cokes at our retail counter, so I took the liberty of putting a couple of Diet Cokes in your fridge, with our compliments." Now *that* would be delightful.

- You can provide enjoyment in a customer experience by doing something good for the customer that was unexpected, also – that is, by providing a pleasant surprise. Because genuine surprises aren't generated by automation, they show that your business has humanity – that it's more than just a smoothly functioning set of processes. As Bill Price and David Jaffe say in their book *Your Customer Rules!*, "What makes surprises so alluring isn't necessarily their content or grandiosity. Even a small kindness, when it's unexpected and freely offered, can change the course of a customer's day. Somehow the unexpected aspect, the surprise, is much more important than the thing itself. Being taken unaware changes the emotional response. The customer is suddenly aware that there are real people on the other side of the transaction, thinking about how to make the day just a little bit better."

Never overlook the human element in a customer experience.

Customer Experience: It's All Relative

To paraphrase Warren Buffett's sidekick Charlie Munger, the secret to a satisfied customer is similar to the secret to a satisfying marriage: low expectations.

As with many things in life, a customer's satisfaction with a product or service is something that can really *only* be measured against that customer's own, personal expectations. The customer will be satisfied with your company's offering if his or her expectations are met. But, of course, this means that if the customer's expectations go up, then satisfying the customer will become more difficult. And the fact is that customer expectations, in general, are a constantly rising tide.

Your customers are not evaluating their customer experience with you against the customer experience delivered by your competitors. They are comparing the customer experience you deliver to the customer experience delivered by Amazon, or JetBlue, or Apple, or American Express.

Claes Fornell is the Swedish professor who came to America more than 20 years ago and founded the American Customer Satisfaction Index (ACSI). In his excellent book, *The Satisfied Customer*, Fornell reports that before field testing the ACSI, his team scoured the literature on customer satisfaction in order to ensure that they captured just the right kind of variables.

According to Fornell,

> *Although there was no consensus on how to measure customer satisfaction, three facets showed up over and over. The most common had to do with the confirmation or disconfirmation of prior expectations. Another was the idea of comparing a company's product to a customer's ideal version of the product—regardless of whether or not such a product even existed. The third facet was the cumulative level of satisfaction when all interactions, the customer's total experience over time with the company, were taken into* account.

In other words, a customer may become less satisfied not because your product or service declines in quality in any way at all, but simply because his or her expectations increase.

Now what do you think is happening to customer expectations, in general, as companies around the world focus more and more on improving the customer experience, streamlining and automating their processes, and constantly improving their online capabilities?

That's right, the general level of customer expectations with regard to all companies is increasing. Which means you can't simply maintain your position by continuing to do what you've always done. If you remain static, your customer satisfaction scores – whether you measure them in terms of ACSI, or NPS, or just some kind of very-happy-to-very-unhappy score – will inevitably decline! In fact, even if you *improve* your service quality, satisfaction may still decline if your improvement isn't keeping up with other companies.

No matter what your business is, no matter what kind of industry or category you dominate today, you simply will not maintain your position, over time, without actively working to improve your customer experience, because the rising tide of customer expectations will soon submerge your satisfaction scores.

And as the pace of technological change continues to accelerate, you can expect to have to improve your customer experience faster and faster, just to keep your head above water.

Putting Humanity into Your Company's Mobile App

Today's customers expect their offline and online experiences with a business to sync up, but in all too many cases they don't. To help meet this challenge, one thing companies will soon begin doing is upgrading their mobile apps to handle real-time, human-to-human customer interactions, no extra call or computer session required.

Imagine the world a few years from now, when your customer will be able to use your company's mobile app to browse for advice about something related to your offer. If she doesn't find the answer to her question, she'll be able to push a button to connect with one of your own live agents (by voice, chat, or video). The agent will see her history on the website and won't require her to repeat everything (the way you have to do today, if you leave a company's website and call in to the toll-free number). When necessary, your agent may even be able to push a diagram of the correct way to operate your product, or a chart of other options available, directly to the customer's smartphone, and all within the same app.

This technology is available today. Already. If you want to deliver a more trustable experience for your own customers, if you want to deliver humanity to your customers directly, then this should be your *company's* app. Today.

Amazon's Mayday button for its Kindle Fire delivers exactly this kind of service. If something goes wrong with your Kindle, or you have trouble figuring out how to do something, you press the Mayday button, and…presto! A real live human being appears on the screen to help you through the problem.

But other companies are now starting to integrate this kind of live, human connection directly into their smartphone apps without requiring a specific device (like the Kindle). At the end of 2014 Weight Watchers, for instance, introduced 24/7 Expert Chat, a feature allowing all premium members to access a live coach anytime, anywhere, for any reason, via chat. And all within the Weight Watchers app itself, whether it was accessed on a computer, a tablet, or a smartphone.

Members get instant advice on how to get started losing weight, or get back on track, or simply stay motivated – 24 hours a day, seven days a week – from a Weight Watchers-certified coach who was once in their shoes and has successfully lost weight. The company has some 16,000 service providers in the field, a significant advantage over its competitors, and at last count it had trained nearly 4,000 of them to connect via the chat app. According to Weight Watchers, voice connections are next.

The company deep-linked this human connection into its mobile app by relying on technology from a start-up named "Humanify," recently spun off from TeleTech. Apps have always been able to "deep link" with other apps. This is why, as John Battelle says in his Searchblog post[11], you get an ad served to you in the middle of your maps function for, say, a nearby restaurant. Battelle says that up to now (late 2014) deep linking has been primarily driven by the commercial incentive to do more cross-selling and lead generation, but he predicts a dramatic change – a "turning point" – coming soon. Deep linking will be used to improve the customer experience, rather than just to boost ad revenues.

This is the frictionless future of the connected customer experience, so watch for the stampede as other brands begin to reach for this kind of drastic improvement in the capabilities of their commercial apps.

CHAPTER 10

It Won't Be Easy

While the idea of managing your customer's experience is compelling (what could be more obvious than trying to watch out for how your customers deal with your product and service?), putting together the resources and processes required to do so is actually quite difficult.

It's difficult for a wide variety of reasons, not the least of which is that your business is almost certainly organized around products, services, and channels, rather than individual customers. It's difficult because it will require capabilities, and technologies, and systems that you probably don't yet have. They're available, that's not in question, but if you haven't already tackled the issue it's highly unlikely you have the required IT systems, software, and tools required. And it's difficult because as compelling as the idea is, it runs counter to how most businesses operate, even today.

So you're likely to run into a buzz saw of resistance when you try to implement the required changes. It definitely won't be easy.

"The More I Buy, the Worse They Treat Me"

This was what a colleague told me about his bank, just the other day.

What he meant was that the more divisions he dealt with at this bank, the less likely any of them would actually know what his total relationship with the bank was like. When he called in about his credit card, for instance, it didn't seem to know he also had checking and money market accounts at their bank.

Then, he said, when he applied for a second mortgage with this bank, it wanted him to fill out all the paperwork first, starting with his name and address, his account numbers, the balances in his accounts, his credit card details, and so forth – all of which was information it had access to (or should have had), because *all these accounts were with this same bank!*

My friend's conclusion: The more he buys from the bank, the more disconnected his experience becomes. All of this bank's various operating units and silos of business may in fact be flying under a single brand name, but they clearly don't talk to each other, and either they don't share a common customer database, or they aren't interested in using it to make their customers' lives simpler. So from the customer's perspective they might as well be entirely separate companies.

In fact, my friend said, it would probably be *better* for him to do business with separate companies, and just manage his finances himself in an integrated way using some online service like Moven or Simple.

This is not a new affliction for business. Many businesses that are made up of separate business units selling their own products or services also have their own marketing and sales functions, funded by the sales they generate for their own units. So these people don't think about the mother ship. They only think about their own division of it.

Sometimes these problems are caused by disconnected IT systems that can't talk to each other in the wake of some merger or business combination. But even then, it's important for a business to pay attention not just to its own operational needs, but also to smoothing the customer experience as much as possible.

If you flew on American Airlines during the year following their purchase of US Airways, for instance, you would have noticed the same kind of disconnected and uncoordinated service. Try to check in for your flight at the airline counter for American, and they would send you to the other end of the check-in area to the US Air counter. Your ticket might have said "American," and your reservation said "American," but rather than telling you in advance that you should check in at the other counter, they let you – the customer – make up for their poor system coordination.

Don't let your own business look like this to customers – like some random bunch of independently operated, uncoordinated companies loosely joined together under some umbrella brand name. Fix your systems or connectivity problems as soon as you can, but until you do fix them, be prepared to provide your customers with a coordinated experience, even if you have to do it manually for a while!

Three Reasons Why Customer Transformations Fail

Is your company engaged in some kind of customer-oriented transformation right now? Perhaps you're facing a threat from a disruptive new online business model in your category, or you have a problem managing individual customer relationships that span different business units, or maybe you're just trying to improve your service and boost your customer satisfaction scores, in order to be more competitively successful.

Whatever your motivation, a customer-centric transformation is a significant undertaking, and many of them just don't succeed. Perhaps as many as two-thirds of these efforts fail, depending on which studies[12] you believe, but regardless of the actual failure rate it can't be denied that making this kind of transformation is extremely difficult.

In my experience counseling companies on this topic over the last 20 years, I've seen three basic kinds of problems that plague a customer transformation:

Lack of Capabilities

Some firms just don't have the right data, systems, analytics, or other technology to track individual customer relationships and manage the customer experience properly. The problem of technical capabilities should be easy to solve, because technology has progressed to such an extent that you can access many of the tools you need via the cloud, with less and less upfront hassle, but more often than not a company doesn't take advantage of the capabilities it would need to address its tech-savvy, 24/7 connected customers.

Which leads to the second problem…

Alignment Issues

When a company's internal goals, metrics, or accountabilities aren't aligned well, they can create conflicts that will undermine any customer-centered initiative. This is what upset my friend when he lamented that none of his bank's various departments – mortgage, credit card, retail checking – seemed to know about his whole relationship with the bank, so the more of the bank's services he used, the less coordinated they seemed. Whenever different business units at a company all sell their own products and services and have their own sales and profit goals, as was apparently the case at this bank, then managing any individual customer's experience across different business units can be difficult.

Or, if a company is simply paying its salespeople commissions to acquire new customers, while at the same time asking the marketing and analytics team to improve customer retention, this will also create a conflict, because the easiest customers for any company to acquire are, by definition, the least loyal. That's why they're easy to acquire.

An alignment problem considerably more difficult to deal with arises when a business tries to reconcile its customer-centric metrics of success (such as customer satisfaction scores) with its own financial metrics and goals. It's fine to set the objective to improve your NPS or your CSAT scores, but when the quarterly profit number is in jeopardy, the vast majority of companies will toss aside this effort if it's necessary to make the number.

Mindset Problems

The third set of obstacles that can make a customer transformation difficult has to do with the mindset of individual employees, from rank-and-file through middle and senior management. The employee has to *want* to delight the customer. But therein lies the problem. Do your employees really have a desire to improve the company's customer experience?

Corporate culture – what employees do when no one is watching – is by far the single most important internal force at any company, for good or bad. As Peter Drucker famously said, "Culture eats strategy for breakfast."

Probably the defining quality in a culture, when it comes to succeeding with a customer-centric transformation, has to do with how individual employees see the company's purpose, or its mission. What do employees consider to be the "direction of success" when they are wrestling with some problem or issue? If the direction of success is always to try to act in the customer's interest, even when it sometimes costs money to do so, this can be a terrifically unifying mission – and it has the added benefit of being something very easy to sell to employees. We're all customers, after all.

And one more thing, very important: Even though the wrong mindset can hinder success, the right kind of mindset can be an enormously valuable asset for overcoming capabilities and alignment problems. If you have a thoroughly engaged and motivated workforce, with a unifying sense of mission that involves acting in the customer's interest, then often your individual employees will act on their own initiative to devise workarounds for a lack of capabilities, or a misalignment of responsibilities.

Do You Allow Employees to Use Common Sense?

You really don't have to *require* employees to be fair to customers. You just have to *let* them.

A few years ago, when my family lived in London, my wife and I were planning a weekend trip to rendezvous with some of our U.S. friends on France's Brittany coast. So she booked a flight to Nantes on British Airways' website in order to arrive about the time everyone else was coming in. Then she called a couple of our friends in the U.S. just to confirm how long everyone was staying, before going back to the website to book her return to London. At this point she learned that a roundtrip ticket bought all at once would have cost less than either of the one-way tickets she was now in the process of buying! Unable to make the correction online, however, she called the British Airways reservations center.

Sorry, the agent replied, nothing could be done. "Your one-way ticket is already booked and paid for. I know it was just an hour ago, but I can't change it now. The system won't let me." My wife asked for the supervisor, but got the same answer, along with a deep, sorrowful apology. "You really are entitled to a refund, and I would definitely issue one if I could. But unfortunately, the company doesn't let us do this, even when it's unfair." The reps my wife talked with about the issue were all in favor of righting this wrong, but they were powerless. And, they seemed personally unhappy with their own company's inflexible rules, as well. In the end, we paid £300 more than we needed to, and we felt cheated.

Fast forward to the next month, when the Family Peppers planned a weekend trip with our two school-age kids to Amsterdam. It was a bank-holiday weekend in the U.K., meaning that Monday was a day off, so we booked four non-refundable roundtrip tickets on EasyJet, a discount airline. But, we were unprepared for the vast amount of traffic leaving London that Friday afternoon and we didn't arrive at Gatwick Airport until 30 minutes after our flight's scheduled departure time. Thoughts going through my head: "This weekend is now completely ruined, because the outbound tickets are nonrefundable, as are the return tickets, the hotel deal in Amsterdam, the whole weekend is shot, this really sucks, etc. etc. etc."

When we arrived at the check-in desk, however, the agent greeted us with a smile, sympathizing with us by saying how easy it is to get tripped up by London traffic. "But, tell you what, why don't you just take a room here at the airport hotel, and I'll waive the re-booking fee and get you out to Amsterdam on our first flight tomorrow morning." Great! We said. "And also," he continued, "give me the name and phone number of the hotel you booked in Amsterdam. I'll call them on your behalf and see if I can get them to waive any charges for tonight."

Now here's the thing. British Airways and EasyJet are both well-run companies with tightly drawn processes. But at British Airways, "system rules" defined all behaviors, and employees were not allowed to exercise their judgment to override the system, even when they knew the system was faulty. The result was a company with ossified, inflexible rules that not only occasionally misfired when it came to customer service, but clearly frustrated the company's own employees, most of whom would have jumped at the chance to deliver a better customer experience.

EasyJet, by contrast, had similar restrictions and rules about its discount fares – even more restrictive in most cases – but the company allowed its employees to use their common sense, and to override those rules (like waiving the rebooking fee) when it was necessary to provide better service.

So here's the question: Which of these airlines' operating styles most closely resembles your own? At your company, how much latitude do you give lower-level employees when it comes to pleasing customers or solving unanticipated (and unscripted) customer problems? And what control or reporting mechanisms do you use to ensure that your employees actually "do the right thing" in handling these kinds of exceptions?

Four Types of Customer Experience to Plan For

You'll never be able to write a line of code or a business process rule that requires an employee to deliver a great customer experience; the employee has to *want* to deliver it.

Sooner or later every company encounters a situation that simply wasn't anticipated in advance. So when a customer's experience involves this kind of unforeseen event, especially if it is of great significance or importance to the customer, you want your employees to be willing and able to deal with it, even if it might mean overriding a standard practice, or making a judgment call on their own authority.

One way to visualize the issue is to use a diagram that categorizes the kind of customer experience you'll be delivering, based on how standardized the business process is for a situation, and how engaged the customer is in it. Based on high and low levels of both process standardization and customer engagement, we can identify four different types of customer experience that must be planned for:

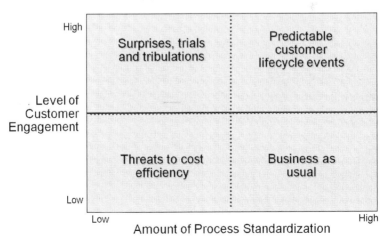

Four Types of Customer Experience

	Low ———— Amount of Process Standardization ———— High
High — Level of Customer Engagement	Surprises, trials and tribulations / Predictable customer lifecycle events
Low	Threats to cost efficiency / Business as usual

The vast majority of customer experiences with any sizable business will be in the lower right quadrant, "Business as usual." Here you have a lot of repetitiveness and a high potential for standardization, while the customer considers the transaction or experience to be routine. Buying one more item from an online retailer, for instance, or making a call to your credit card company to check your balance, are business-as-usual customer experiences. And many of these kinds of experiences can be entirely automated, which gives the company the ability to deliver a completely frictionless experience simply by hard-wiring the right customer-centric processes into its computer system. When iTunes reminds you that you already bought an item you're about to purchase, it's not because anyone made an on-the-spot decision about how to treat you, but because it anticipated the situation in advance and built appropriate rules into its computer system.

In the upper right quadrant, "Predictable customer lifecycle events," the customer experience is highly significant in the customer's mind, but it is still predictable, and the delivery of that experience can be standardized, even though customers themselves are likely to be highly interested or engaged in them, and would probably not think of them as routine. One example might be when a customer receives his very first bill from the mobile carrier he just signed up with. He's likely to be quite interested in understanding why the bill is higher than he had expected, and in many cases he'll call the carrier to discuss it. But, because all new customers receive a first invoice at some point, and it's not uncommon for them to call in to inquire about it, the mobile company can prepare for this customer experience in advance. It will likely have a standardized way to deal with these kinds of inquiries.

In the lower left quadrant, "Threats to cost efficiency" are many of the kinds of customer experiences that weren't anticipated and planned for already, including unusual requests or out of the ordinary events, in which the customer isn't terribly interested or engaged. Your company still has to pay attention to them, however, and manually address these issues one at a time, because they undermine your cost efficiency. An example might be, for instance, when a hotel company's website can't automatically consolidate a customer's duplicate frequent guest accounts because of an overlooked discrepancy in the address field, or some other minor problem. For the most part this is nuisance friction, and you should be logging each such problem as it comes up, in order to continually improve your process standardization and automation capabilities.

It's in the upper left quadrant, however, where a negative customer experience can be the most threatening to a company's profitability and reputation. The customer experience in this quadrant is one in which the customer is highly engaged, but the company itself has not prepared in advance to address the issue, and there is no standardized process in place. This might be because the problem was hard to anticipate in advance, or because the company hasn't been careful enough in mapping out all its customer journeys to begin with. Either way, these "surprises, trials, and tribulations" will test a firm's corporate culture.

So the question for your company is, when a customer is wronged or ill-served in some way, how easily can the situation be remedied by rank-and-file employees who get involved in the customer's interaction?

The vast majority of employees – and particularly those in customer service jobs – *want* to work for a company that can be trusted by its customers. But if you want to be able to handle the kinds of problems encountered in this upper left quadrant effectively, then your employees must be (1) actively engaged with your firm and its mission, and (2) enabled to make the decisions and take action on their own.

Dealing With the Alignment Problem

"We have met the enemy and he is us."

– Pogo

Whenever companies try to improve their customer service and become more customer-centric, one of the first and most important problems they confront almost always has to do with how well their internal metrics and responsibilities are aligned with the goal of being customer-centric. In most cases they aren't, and this misalignment represents an existential threat to whatever customer-oriented activities are being planned.

On a business trip not long ago I met individually with senior executives at several large and successful companies. Each of these companies had a brand name that was virtually a household word in its market, and each had already publicly declared its strong commitment toward better customer service.

The commitment went by different names at these firms – "Customer Advocacy," "Service Revolution," "Customer Transformation," or "Customer Excellence" – but the bottom line was that each firm was sincerely focused on improving its own customers' experiences with its brand. This is an admirable goal, and it is something that an increasing number of companies are committing to, because customer service can, in fact, be a very powerful competitive differentiator.

The companies I met with were in a variety of industries, including financial services, telecommunications, media, and technology, and they had made different amounts of progress toward their goal. But what struck me was what they all had in common. They each confronted almost the exact same roadblock to further progress, and it was a self-inflicted wound.

The roadblock confronting each of these firms was that being more customer-centric conflicted with the fundamental alignment of the organization. It interfered with how success was actually measured and rewarded, and with how responsibilities were allocated among various executives and departments.

At one large financial services firm, I had an hour-long conversation with a very senior executive who appealed to me over and over again to please tell her how it could do better. Toward the end of our discussion, however, I only had to point out that each and every problem she had identified was internal to her company and could be remedied with a change in policy. For instance, although she desperately wanted her firm to treat customers better, at the end of every quarter she said her people had to hustle just to achieve their financial goals, which undermined customer service. To make the top-line numbers they often had to sell whatever they could to whatever customers they could sell to, despite their carefully laid plans to treat each customer more appropriately and individually, based on individual customer interests. And to make their bottom-line numbers they sometimes resorted to clamping down on many of the more costly customer service initiatives, which led to a stop-and-go kind of unpredictability in their policies.

At another firm, a telecom company's CEO and senior staff had committed heavily and publicly to raising their firm's level of customer service. It turned out that because the numbers were not being achieved in one recent quarter, the finance department unilaterally decided to impose a tight limitation on customer refunds. The new policy was so strict that it made it difficult for a customer to get a refund at all, no matter how severely disrupted his or her service was. This was a significant change to the prior refund policy and, naturally, it completely undermined the customer service initiative.

No matter what you call your own company's customer-oriented initiative, you won't make much progress until you firmly *commit* to aligning your company's financial-centric and customer-centric metrics of success. The most straightforward way to do this, in my view, is to spend time and effort documenting the fact that the customer base itself is a valuable corporate asset, and that good service will increase its value, while bad service will diminish it.

Customers create two kinds of value at a firm – short-term value when they buy something, and long-term value when they have a good experience, which increases their lifetime value. Whether or not your firm actually employs sophisticated analytics to model the lifetime values of different kinds of customers, it can't be denied that these lifetime values do, in fact, exist. Nor can it be denied that a customer's lifetime value will go up or down as the customer's attitude toward a brand improves or declines. The financial asset value of your customer base – often called "customer equity" – is simply the sum total of lifetime values of all your current and future customers.

Ideally, if you want to beat the alignment problem at your own firm, you should commit to a customer analytics effort sufficient to begin gauging which service improvements tend to generate what kinds of lifetime value increases, and which service problems tend to generate what kinds of lifetime value decreases.

If you find this analytics task too complicated or difficult, then at a bare minimum you need to persuade your investors, your board, and your senior executives that any financial metrics that ignore the asset value of the customer base entirely (as almost all current financial metrics do) are fundamentally flawed. They simply don't paint an accurate picture of your company's true financial prospects.

One quick fix for the problem would be to assign financial values to whatever non-financial customer-centric metrics you are tracking. Make your best, most reasonable estimate, but in the end just make the arbitrary assumption that an increase of x percent in average customer satisfaction, for instance, is worth a y percent increase in customer equity.

If you're a senior executive wrestling with the difficulty of gaining traction for your own company's customer initiative, my advice is to focus carefully on fixing the alignment problem, before it completely undermines even your most enlightened customer experience improvement efforts.

The Alignment Problem Up Close and Personal

A friend of mine makes a decent living working at a contact center where for years the primary activity has been fielding inbound calls from retail customers interested in buying one or more of the firm's high-end products.

Not long ago, however, this firm decided it should be doing a better job of managing relationships with its customers, so it introduced CRM software to begin tracking callers and the sales reps they talk to. They wanted a record of each customer's information, along with a synopsis of each call and its results. My friend, who is a firm believer in the power of relationships to build sales, was part of the pilot program that introduced the system.

But he told me the system didn't work very well when it was implemented, because the salespeople at the call center were undermining the company's objective, which just didn't align with their own objectives (to maximize their commission income).

The company wanted salespeople to begin cultivating relationships with past buyers, because if reps maintained relationships they would generate more customer loyalty and future sales. So to ensure that its reps did this, the company began requiring everyone to make at least 12 outbound contacts per day with customers they'd handled sales for in the past – that is, with the customers who were allocated to them by the CRM system, based on past transactions. And under the rules of this quota system, only a voice contact was to be counted. It wouldn't be sufficient for a rep to make 12 attempts – he or she had to *reach* 12 folks on the phone, which usually meant making 20 to 30 additional attempts, and would often consume an hour or more of a rep's day.

According to my friend, the company's managers were soon puzzled by the fact that the CRM system wasn't producing the results it had hoped for, even after implementing this policy. There was no noticeable uptick in sales and, if anything, the reps' productivity numbers declined after implementing this set of processes.

The problem was that this company's call-center reps were all commissioned salespeople who lived and died by the sales they made. By requiring them to take time out of their day to accomplish one more task – making a certain number of outbound contacts – the company was reducing the time they had available to field inbound calls and make more commissions for themselves.

The reps quickly figured out that making contacts with previous customers and trying to get them to buy something more was not a very promising idea, when there were calls coming in all the time that could generate commissions *right now*. Building a longer-term relationship with a past customer would only pay off for a rep much later, if at all.

So to minimize the time required to make these dozen outbound contacts, many of the reps didn't try to make contact with the folks who had bought the most expensive or comprehensive product package the last time around. While these were obviously the company's best customers, based on history, they also tended to be much more difficult to reach on the phone. Instead, the reps would call as many small-purchase, easily reachable people as possible, even though they knew they wouldn't be selling anything to them. They just want to "check the box" as fast as possible and get back to answering the phone. And earning commissions.

For a company wanting to strengthen its customer relationships, there's an important lesson here. You can't "install" customer relationships with new CRM technology. Nor can you simply decree that employees should engage customers in relationships for the long-term benefit of the company. Your employees have to *want* to do it.

Six Leadership Behaviors for a Customer-Centric Transformation

Because new technologies have armed today's customers with up-to-the-minute information about the companies they buy from, the products they want, and the opinions of their friends and acquaintances about each brand's customer experience, there's hardly a business anywhere that isn't trying to become more customer-centric.

I was once asked to run a workshop for a small group of senior executives at a large, multi-division enterprise seeking to transform itself into a more customer-centric business. During a planning call with the company's CEO, he asked me how he would know whether the workshop was a success.

What do you mean? I asked.

Well, he said, what will my executives do differently, if we're successful at convincing them that this is a good direction for our company?

It was a good question, so we brainstormed the issue on the phone for a few minutes, trying to list the kinds of "leadership behaviors" that would be expected of an executive who became convinced that moving his or her company in a more customer-centric direction was the right course. And, with only a few modifications I've been using this list of leadership behaviors in my workshops and speeches for a number of years now.

If, after reading the essays in this book, you want to ensure that your own company becomes more capable of delivering a genuinely satisfying customer experience, then here are six "leadership behaviors" to watch for among your managers:

Accumulating expertise in customer centricity. Leaders committed to improving the customer experience will do things like attend conferences and training sessions, benchmark with customer-centric firms, and share best practices with other business units or affiliated companies. If I see leaders setting up and participating in customer-oriented training programs for employees, for instance, then I know their commitment to their company's transformation is genuine. (Reading this book is a good start.)

Making direct, insight-generating contact with customers, regularly. Leaders committed to delivering a better customer experience will demand more voice-of-customer feedback. They'll crave it. This might mean attending focus groups and research sessions personally, or interviewing customers directly. It could involve mystery shopping their own firm, as well as their competitors' firms. At a B2B company, where regular contacts between salespeople and customers are the rule, what I would look for would be higher-quality contacts – discussions, not about the products the company has on offer, but about the business problems or issues the customer is encountering.

Crossing boundaries to generate enterprisewide results. Organizational silos are anathema when it comes to customer centricity, so leaders who are committed to a better customer experience will spend the time and effort necessary to break them down. But even when these barriers persist, committed leaders will do their best to ensure that each customer has an experience that is consistent across all products and channels. When they commit to this kind of transformation, leaders will make it their business to sponsor cross-departmental initiatives aimed at eliminating inconsistencies and sharing best practices.

Measuring success differently. Crossing boundaries can only be effective over the long term if new metrics and reward structures are also introduced, including things like customer satisfaction scores and NPS. The benefits of better service or higher customer satisfaction often don't translate into sales and profit in the current financial period, so when a firm's incentive compensation plans are based solely on financial performance, I know the firm's leaders aren't truly committed to customer centricity. They may consider it nice to have, but not essential. Customer centricity requires a company to link financial incentives and budgeting decisions to the metrics gauging the quality of the customer experience, it's that simple. For example, one of our large technology clients (which I'm not allowed to name) retained us to help generate sales to small and medium business customers. However, the primary metric for rewarding our success in this contract isn't sales volume, but customer satisfaction scores. This client's leaders are authentically committed to delivering a quality customer experience.

170

Focusing on incremental progress and "quick wins." A large part of any change management effort at a company will involve accumulating small successes, celebrating them, and building gradual organizational momentum toward the change required. To be successful, a company's leaders must not be so consumed with the ultimate destination that they can't pay attention to fixing small problems, getting bite-sized projects off the ground, and piloting a variety of customer-centric initiatives in different areas, simultaneously. The competitive world changes too quickly to wait for perfect solutions. But over time small efforts, limited-scope projects, quick wins, and even "near misses" all add to the momentum. This makes it easier to attempt, justify, and implement larger efforts, and it builds support for the direction of change among the rank-and-file.

Communicating and living by customer-centric values. Finally, does your executive team really "walk the walk" or just "talk the talk" about delivering a good customer experience? A committed leader finds opportunities to discuss with staff members how the company should treat certain *types* of customers, perhaps focusing on particular lifestyles, transaction patterns, or just simple demographics. He or she will place greater emphasis on initiatives designed to improve the different customer experiences among a variety of different types of customers. And a leader committed to customer centricity will also be committed to transparency and trust – ensuring that the organization's official policy is always to act in the customer's interest, even when it might not yield the same level of short-term profit.

CHAPTER 11

There's Real Money to Be Made

Business is not a charity. To stay in business, a company needs to earn a profit.

One of the most difficult issues to resolve, when putting together a program designed to raise the quality of your customer experience, is how to pay for it. Delivering better service costs money, so where will that money come from, and will you ever get it back?

The fact is that customers may be the single most important asset that your business has. This wasn't always the case. As recently as 1980, virtually 100 percent of the market capitalization of the S&P 500 was in the form of tangible assets – plants, inventories, and other *things*. But in a dramatic change, by 2010 only 40 percent of the S&P 500 market cap was in the form of tangible assets. The rest was a hodgepodge of what accountants call "good will," but what could easily be called "customer equity." Apple, Google, Facebook, and Microsoft together are worth nearly $2 trillion, and the vast majority of this value comes from their customer franchise, not their facilities, and not even their patents.

The trick to profiting from providing a better customer experience isn't creating value. It's reconciling the value your customers create for you with outdated accounting conventions that have yet to catch up with the changes that technology has wrought.

How to Pay For a Better Customer Experience

Everyone agrees that a better customer experience should be good for a company, but a lot of us worry about how to pay for it. Customer service does cost money, so the question is how to tell whether the cost of delivering a better experience is worth it or not. Will a better customer experience pay for itself?

At Amazon, the most useful indicator of a customer's satisfaction is considered to be "resolution." The company wants to ensure that all of a customer's problems are quickly and easily resolved, so that no friction interferes with any customer's experience. According to one former Amazon executive, the single most important metric it uses to gauge success in its own call centers is what it calls the Negative Resolution Rate, or NRR.

While most call centers track metrics like average handle time (AHT) and first-call resolution (FCR), Amazon goes directly to the issue of customer dissatisfaction. NRR is specifically designed to track any friction in the customer experience that has yet to be eliminated – friction that inevitably generates unhappiness, frustration, or even anger in the customer's mind.

To improve its customer experience, Amazon focuses relentlessly on the problems encountered and not yet completely resolved. It keeps those problems visible to the enterprise until they are fixed, and then tries to ensure that similar problems don't arise.

Seeking out and eliminating the sources of friction will often pay for your customer experience improvement just by reducing the costs involved in handling these unresolved problems, one problem at a time. You don't have to boil the ocean to improve your customer experience; you don't even have to heat up the pond.

Want an example? Consider how Fidelity's SVP of Customer Experience, Parrish Arturi, approached the problem. As recounted by Forrester's Harley Manning and Kerry Bodine in their book *Outside In*, Arturi focused his efforts on one small process improvement at a time. Importantly, he set up a customer experience improvement budget and allowed people to tap it for small amounts of funds to fix these individual problems without having to do fully fleshed out proposals.

Manning and Bodine recount one instance of how this operated:

> *One of these small projects began when a service rep noticed that a large number of people were having trouble logging in to their accounts through an automated phone system. The rep started a thread about the situation on a Fidelity discussion board dedicated to generating ideas for experience improvements. [Arturi's] team, the owners of the board, saw the thread and flagged it for attention, [and]... then worked with the people who manage the phone system to identify the root cause of the login issue and quickly launch a solution.*
>
> *Although the total cost of that fix was less than $20,000, it saves Fidelity $4 million a year by averting calls to customer service. It was just one of over 160 projects that came through Fidelity's experience improvement system in 2011. Together those projects accounted for over $24 million in annual savings.*

You could do this for your own company, couldn't you? Establish a small budget of funds for the specific purpose of removing the points of friction in your customer experience. Then let your employees – even rank-and-file workers – tap this fund for small amounts without having to submit comprehensive proposals to senior people.

And watch your customer experience get better, one resolved problem at a time.

Customers Create Two Kinds of Value

I'm a lifelong runner. And whether racing or training, when I want to increase my speed there are only two options: I can try to pick up my pace by taking quicker steps, or I can try to lengthen my stride by covering more ground with each step. But these two methods conflict with each other. When I quicken my pace it's more difficult to take bigger strides, and when I lengthen my stride it's harder to take faster steps.

A similar conflict exists with how a business handles the quality of the customer experience it delivers. Customers create value for a business in two different ways: They buy more today, or they improve their disposition toward you and buy more tomorrow. But for a business these two types of value creation are fundamentally in conflict just like pace and stride are in conflict for a runner. The harder you work to "sell" a customer on today's offering, the more likely you are to wear out your welcome and erode the customer's willingness to buy in the future.

The biggest problem facing businesses today, I believe, is that most are so totally focused on short-term results that they are unable to see this trade-off for what it is – a trade-off. Companies find it easy to count each period's sales and convert this to a financial value, but it isn't so easy to quantify the financial value of improving the customer experience.

This doesn't mean it can't be done at all – just that it's a bit more difficult. In economic terms, the financial value of future cash flows attributable to a customer is the customer's lifetime value (LTV). So when a business improves a customer's predisposition to buy in the future, or to recommend the business to other customers, it is increasing the customer's LTV. The *increase* in a customer's LTV produced by a better customer experience is real economic value created today. But the cash effect of that increase in value won't be realized until sometime in the future.

Another way to think about it is to visualize the cost of a bad customer experience. Suppose a good customer calls you with a complaint, and for some reason your firm doesn't handle the complaint very well, so at the end of the call this very valuable customer slams the phone down in disgust. Didn't your firm just lose a little bit of its economic value, as a going business? Economically, the value of your business is the net present value of the future cash flow you expect to generate, but the future cash flow you can expect now has diminished somewhat, because this customer will buy less, and perhaps a few of his friends or colleagues might buy less, as well.

So the event that destroyed this economic value occurred *today*, with the customer's lousy customer experience, but the actual cash effect of this event won't be realized until some point in the future. And therein lies the problem for most businesses.

If you don't make some attempt to measure your customers' lifetime values and try to understand today's events that cause these values to increase or decrease, your business is doomed to live perpetually in the world of short-termism. Competitively you'll be prey to other companies that take a longer-term view of their business, and try to strike a balance that generates *both* kinds of value.

Unlike products, customers have memories, which means that customer relationships are the most direct link between a company's short-term financial results and its long-term shareholder value.

How Do You Build the Business Case for a Good Customer Experience?

Let's face it: If delivering a better customer experience were *always* beneficial to a company's bottom line, then there would never be any question about how to fund the effort.

A better experience will encourage customers to come back more often, spend more, and refer their friends, all of which will benefit future sales. But these future benefits must be weighed against the costs of providing that better customer experience to begin with. Good service isn't free, so the question is how much are you willing to spend to secure how much increase in future sales?

The difficulty most companies come up against when trying to evaluate the business case for delivering a better customer experience comes from the fact that while the increased *cost* of a better experience can easily be measured, the *benefits* it will generate occur sometime in the future, and can only be guessed at.

If you've sometimes struggled with this issue, here are some ideas for assessing the business case for delivering a better customer experience:

Run an A/B test

Before undertaking a costly improvement in service across your whole customer base, test it on some statistically representative sample of customers. Then measure their future transactions, compared to those who weren't given the better service.

Running a test is straightforward, but you'd be surprised how few managers actually employ A/B testing to make better business decisions[13].

Testing a service improvement against a baseline of normal service requires you to run the test for a long enough period to be able to estimate the actual future behavior of the customers exposed to it. For instance, a few years ago when a book club decided that making "welcome calls" to new customers tended to increase first-year sales by 8 percent and annual renewals by 6 percent, it had to track customer behaviors for at least a year following the calls to find this out.

In some situations, it won't be practical to run an A/B test, because you can't set up a statistically valid control population. In addition, to run a test, your customers have to be individually addressable. That's why you can't really test a broadcast radio or television ad, for instance (although you can test different ads in different geographical areas).

Use "Return on Customer" as a metric

If you calculate, track, and fully analyze your customer lifetime values, you should eventually be able to measure your actual Return on Customer for various service initiatives. Return on Customer (ROC) differs from return on investment (ROI) because it uses customer lifetime values in the denominator of the fraction, rather than total dollars invested. And at the enterprise level, ROC is mathematically equivalent to Total Shareholder Return.

Companies that engage in continuous predictive modeling of customer behaviors (as some of the more sophisticated telecom and financial services firms do) will be able, over time, to identify and quantify leading indicators of lifetime value change. For instance, you may find that when customer satisfaction, NPS, or some other survey-based gauge of customer attitude increases by X points, within a certain segment of customers, it might predict an increase of $Y in customer lifetime values within that segment. This kind of insight – which can be developed over years of tracking individual customer behaviors in a variety of segments – will allow you to estimate the *future* financial benefit of a service improvement by measuring the *current* improvement in surveyed customer attitudes. (For more about the benefits and limitations of this metric, see Martha Rogers' and my book on the subject, *Return on Customer: Creating Maximum Value From Your Scarcest Resource.*)

Use non-financial metrics

Obviously, you can't make a "business case" without using financial metrics. But if your company is forward-thinking enough to realize that the financial metrics produced by most businesses today are woefully inadequate when it comes to capturing all the value-creating and value-destroying actions that any business engages in, then you might already be using a number of non-financial metrics to assess the performance of various departments or initiatives.

Your customer service center, for instance, might be evaluated not just on the average cost or time required to handle an incoming call (which correlates to short-term cost), but on the percentage of inquiries completely answered on a single call, or perhaps on the level of customer satisfaction measured (which correlates with changes in lifetime value). These would be non-financial metrics.

Measuring the ROI of a Frictionless Customer Experience

A man was visiting his farmer friend one weekend, and as the two of them sat in rocking chairs on the front porch the visitor couldn't help but notice a pig hobbling around the barnyard with a wooden leg. How remarkable! So, he asked his host, what's the story on that pig with a wooden leg there?

Oh, the farmer replied, that's my pig Winslow. Winslow is one terrific pig. We had a barn fire about a year ago and believe it or not, Winslow went into the barn and dragged my two-year-old son Jimmy out by the scruff of his neck. Probably saved Jimmy's life.

So, the visitor surmised. Winslow must have injured his leg in the fire?

No, the farmer said, but when you have something that good, you only want to eat it a little at a time.

A lot of businesses today generate their profits by eating their own customers a little at a time. Response rates continue to decline generally, across all forms of outbound marketing, while customers themselves feel less loyal to the brands they deal with, so their lifetime values are declining, as well. Why?

It's really very simple. The overwhelming majority of businesses measure their financial success based on current sales and costs, while customers are focused on the customer experience they anticipate.

The ROI of delivering a frictionless customer experience isn't reflected in a company's current-period sales. When a customer has a frictionless experience she becomes less likely to defect and more likely to buy things in the future, but the cash effect of these benefits won't be realized until some financial period in the future. They represent an increase in the customer's current lifetime value, but not in her current purchasing.

The problem is that there is an inherent conflict – a trade-off – between a customer's current-period purchases and her lifetime value. For one thing, successive outbound marketing campaigns will inevitably suffer from diminishing returns, as the most likely customers buy first, so the population of remaining customers becomes less and less likely to buy. But in addition, the more aggressively a business tries to promote its current sales, the more resistant its customers will become, perhaps even feeling pressured and losing trust in the marketer's motives.

Most companies don't have analytics systems refined and ambitious enough to estimate the magnitude of an increase in a customer's lifetime value, so they ignore it altogether. Instead, they focus solely on the dollars and cents involved in this quarter's transactions. They are laboring under the ridiculous idea that the more easily measured something is, the more important it must be.

The result is that almost all large businesses are maniacally obsessed with short-term results, primarily because they are the easiest results to measure. If your business is operating this way, here are a few things you can do to ensure that your efforts to deliver a better customer experience don't fall victim to short-termism:

- Improve your customer analytics function to ensure that average customer lifetime value is regularly measured (at least quarterly, if not daily) for a variety of different customer segments.

- Then track *changes* in lifetime value over time, in order to understand the actual financial value created by improvements or changes in the delivered customer experience. (Use test-and-control mechanisms to try to eliminate, as far as possible, non-relevant factors.)

- Introduce some non-financial metrics of success, in addition to the financial metrics of sales revenue, costs, and profits. NPS, customer satisfaction scores, and other voice-of-customer metrics can be correlated with changes in customer lifetime values. Over time this will give you a useful "shortcut" for estimating the real ROI of improvements in the customer experience.

- Be sure to get the CEO's commitment to this effort, and explain the program to shareholders. Otherwise, these kinds of metrics will get thrown out again the very first time your company's short-term results decline.

If you continue to focus entirely on current-period financial results, you will be gradually depleting the customer lifetime values available to your business.

And, you really don't want to be in the business of eating your own customers, a little at a time.

The Business Benefit of Being Trustable

When you build a home to sell to someone else in Connecticut (and in many other states) you're required to guarantee the structure and its construction quality for 12 months. During this warranty period, the builder is required to fix all structural flaws or defects at his own expense.

A number of years ago, my wife and I had a house built in Connecticut. What surprised me was that a few months after we moved in to it I got a call from our builder reminding me that my warranty period was going to be up soon (I had forgotten all about it). He said he would be happy to send a team over to examine our house for any defects, in order to ensure that they would be repaired within the warranty period, at the builder's expense.

This is the essence of what it means to be trustable – treating the customer the way you'd like to be treated yourself, if you were the customer. It's obvious that when you do this, your customers will want to buy more, because it's always in their interest to deal with you.

But homebuilding is a business with very few repeat customers, and a builder won't gain much financial benefit from customer loyalty. So I asked our builder why he undertook this service. I greatly appreciated it, but it obviously cost him money, relative to the alternative of just sitting quietly by while the majority of clients forgot about their warranties.

He told me he does it because he generates referrals of new customers at about twice the rate as his competitors do, and referrals represent a very substantial portion of any homebuilder's business. In addition, he has an easier time hiring new employees, because employees themselves *want* to work for his kind of business. It makes them feel better, knowing that they are always trying to do what's in their customers' interest.

Because customers remember you, when you treat customers to a good customer experience today, they will remember this in the future, and they'll likely change their future behavior. Perhaps they'll do more business with you, or they'll refer friends and acquaintances to you. And demonstrating selfless trustability has to be one of the most direct routes to a better customer experience.

It is the customer experience that provides the "missing link" between your company's short-term, current-period earnings and its long-term, ongoing value as a business enterprise – its shareholder value. If you want to build your own shareholder value, think of all the opportunities you might find, just by helping your customers avoid oversights. In addition to warning customers when their warranty period is about to expire:

- Send customers an email reminder before charging their credit card to renew an annual subscription.

- Advise customers proactively if they are overlooking a less expensive or more appropriate option.

- Remind customers by SMS or email a few days before a late fee would apply to their payment.

- Warn customers when it appears they are about to buy more than they likely need.

- Proactively notify customers when they've become eligible for a product upgrade or for a higher-value service.

CHAPTER 12

How Much Is Customer Loyalty Really Worth?

You can buy a customer's loyalty but you have to earn the customer's satisfaction.

I've always had mixed feelings about the issue of customer "loyalty," because for many businesses what they actually mean by the term isn't the affection and goodwill of a customer, but simply the customer's repeat business. Period.

Repeat business is certainly an important financial contributor to a company's success, but it shouldn't be confused with the kind of trust and affection that genuinely *loyal* customers will have for a brand they consider to be "theirs."

And customer trust? Now that's worth real money.

Customer Retention Should Never Be Your Only Goal

No matter what your business is, I can absolutely guarantee you an increase in your average customer retention rate. If customer retention is the only thing you care about, I have a 100 percent sure-fire method to improve it, no matter how good or how bad your product or service is, and no matter how many customers you have today.

Want to know my secret? Just stop acquiring new customers. That's right, quit bringing on any new customers and it's a mathematical certainty that your average customer retention rate will increase.

The reason is very simple. In any given population of customers, different customers will always have different likelihoods of remaining loyal. Some are more prone to defection than others, and they're more likely to leave first. So the customers who remain, on average, will consist more and more of those who were less likely to leave to begin with. It's a statistical certainty that your newest customers will be less likely to stay loyal, on average, than those who have already been with you for a longer period.

Of course, my foolproof method for improving average customer loyalty is not really a sound business strategy, because over time your business will die if you don't recruit any new customers. No business can remain healthy without new customers.

I'm using this as just one more illustration of the importance of thinking about your sales and marketing objectives in a balanced way. Long-term value creation is just as important as short-term sales. And customer acquisition should be balanced with customer retention. The next time you hear someone brag that their average customer retention has increased, be sure to ask them whether customer acquisitions increased or decreased during the same period. And if they don't know the answer to that question, or don't understand why it's important, then they don't really understand what happened to their customer retention rate at all, do they?

In fact, the best way to discuss customer retention, as a percentage rate metric, is to refer to it as a percent of all customers in a particular "vintage" (customers acquired in Year 1, Year 2, Year 3, etc.), or in a specific "cohort" (customers acquired in Campaign A, or Campaign B, or Initiative C, etc.).

But there's another lesson here, as well. Whatever your customer acquisition strategy, it's important to take into account the simple fact that some customers are naturally more likely to remain loyal than others, and to appeal specifically to those types of customers, whenever possible. As I mentioned in a previous essay, this was the strategy Lexus pursued in its early days, and the result is that Lexus continues to have one of the highest customer loyalty rates in the automotive category.

Here are a few additional ideas:

- Design your sales incentives to reflect more than one-size-fits-all customer acquisition. You might consider paying a higher commission for certain types of customers than others, or perhaps providing a salesperson with a continuing revenue stream for ongoing business. Imagine how a car dealership might operate, for instance, if it gave salespeople commissions not just based on the initial sale of a car, but perhaps a small percentage of whatever additional business the customer generates over the next several years (including service visits, other cars, referrals, etc.).

- Put a value proposition together that is more appealing to the most knowledgeable customers. These are the customers more likely to have high word-of-mouth influence with others.

- In the B2B space, focus hard on acquiring "good" customers, as opposed to other types of customers. You want to zero in on the kinds of customers more likely to want suppliers capable of adding value, rather than simply slashing costs to the bare minimum.

- Offer customers the opportunity to help other customers with service or usage issues, not just to gain value from the goodwill of your more loyal customers, but also to improve their commitment to the brand.

- Renounce the short-termism that forces you to focus only on immediate, easily measurable numbers such as sales and costs (and the average retention rate), in order to take into account long-term and non-financial metrics as well, such as lifetime values and customer satisfaction levels.

When Are Loyalty Programs a Waste of Money?

Cost cutting and streamlining are always compelling business strategies. Occasionally, business executives have second thoughts about their loyalty programs and ask our consultants whether their program is really worth its cost.

The answer, however, depends on how well the program is aligned with the type of customer base being served.

A loyalty program or frequent-buyer program rewards customers with points, miles, or other credits that can be redeemed for discounts and free products. Loyalty programs have become ubiquitous in a variety of industries, from airlines and groceries to credit cards, soft drinks, packaged goods, mobile phone services, coffee and restaurant chains, and retailers of all kinds. But they are probably over-used; in the U.S. alone, researchers have tallied more than 2 billion loyalty program memberships, which means the average U.S. household belongs to about 18 different programs.

And they do cost money, not just in terms of the rewards and prizes offered, but also the administrative burden, so it's not uncommon for executives to question their value. Evaluating a program, however, should be based on the circumstances under which it will generate incremental repeat business, and how valuable its other benefits are, including the chance to gain insight into individual customer needs and preferences.

In 1996, Martha Rogers and I published our second book together, *Enterprise One to One*, and we tackled the first question head on. We hypothesized that a loyalty program is probably more efficient at boosting customer retention whenever a business' customer base has two specific characteristics:

1. Just a few high-value customers do the vast majority of business; and

2. Customers' needs are fairly uniform, so that there isn't much product differentiation in the category.

(Fifteen years following the publication of our book, two Yale marketing professors, K. Sudhir and Jiwoong Shin, were given the John D. C. Little Award in marketing science for having proved Martha's and my argument mathematically.)

The long and the short of it is that paying customers for their loyalty is more likely to generate a direct profit when your customers have similar needs but highly different values. The airline industry is a great example. At a typical airline, the top 1 percent or so of flyers account for a much larger percentage of flights sold, and probably generate a majority of its profits. But all the airline's customers are fairly uniform in their needs—to get safely and reliably from Point A to Point B—and pretty much any airline that flies that route can do the trick. There's little demand for any particular seat or service on board a flight, because all the passengers in any class of service receive basically the same treatment.

So airlines benefit by using a loyalty program to purchase customer loyalty directly, but if your business isn't characterized by a similar kind of customer base, with a small minority of extremely high-value consumers who have relatively undifferentiated needs, then it might not make as much sense for you.

Which brings us to the second issue: What other business benefits can a loyalty program generate? One benefit central to the majority of retailers' loyalty programs has to do with compiling and using customer-specific data. By encouraging customers to identify themselves (in order to get their benefits), you can track their purchases and interactions, and then use insights from this data to tailor your offer, your product, or your service to individual tastes. In effect, rather than rewarding customers for their patronage, you're rewarding them for identifying themselves.

This strategy, however, is the most compelling not only when you have no natural mechanism for linking customers' purchases with their identities, but also when your customers are highly diverse in their needs, so that understanding different customers' needs can be used to construct different offers and sales propositions for different customers.

Grocery retailing is a good example here. The typical U.S. grocery store has roughly 40,000 different SKUs (stock-keeping units) on its shelves. But the average household will buy less than 1 percent of them, and every shopper buys a different assortment. So individual customers' types, sizes, and brand preferences vary quite widely. Moreover, unless shoppers somehow identify themselves at the cash register, the grocer has no practical way to keep a record of any individual shopper's purchases. By using a loyalty program to identify individual customers and track each customer's transactions, however, a grocer can compile enough data to make personally relevant offers.

Consum, a Spanish supermarket chain with more than 2 million loyalty program customers, offers printable customized coupons directly from store kiosks, using purchase data to print the right coupons to the right individual. The company turned 12 percent of their loyal customers into monthly users of the kiosks, with some stores reaching 25 percent. And the program generated an 8 percent increase in incremental sales.

So if you want to avoid wasting money on your company's loyalty program, ask yourself these questions:

How much of your business comes from the top 1 percent or 2 percent of your customers?

Is it possible to identify and track your customers' individual purchases even without a loyalty program?

Do your customers have diverse needs and preferences?

Are you prepared, organizationally, to treat different customers differently?

Loyalty Programs Provide "Longitudinal Insight"

For many businesses, one of the most significant benefits provided by a loyalty program is tracking the purchases made by individual customers, over time. This generates what you might call "longitudinal insight" into customer behaviors. All marketers need longitudinal insight to see how their business is actually affected by the experiences their customers have with them, but some business models won't naturally provide that insight without a tool like a loyalty program.

If you operate a chain of retail stores, for instance, your customers come in and buy your products, pay for them at the cash register, and leave. Without a loyalty program or some other customer-specific mechanism (for instance, a membership requirement), you have no way to connect a customer's purchases today with what that particular customer purchased yesterday, or last week, or last year.

So let's say your merchandising manager wants to evaluate how much shelf space is allocated to various products carried in the store. She'd like to increase the space provided for her most profitable products by trimming the space given to her least profitable products. To make this decision, she relies on your point-of-sale (POS) data. The problem is, while POS data will give her an accurate snapshot of sales at any one point in time, the data won't show how any individual customer's purchases have varied over time.

To see how crippling this is, suppose the POS data your merchandising manager sees for three different products stocked in one category look like this:

	Weekly Units	Weekly Spend	Total Stores	Spend per Store
Product A	10350	$ 26,393	267	$ 99
Product B	6300	$ 17,010	210	$ 81
Product C	5100	$ 10,965	166	$ 66

From this table of data, it certainly appears as if Product A is your best seller. At $99 per store, each week it generates 50 percent more revenue than Product C, while Product B is somewhere in between. This is a snapshot of the average week's sales, and if any product ought to be de-emphasized or even discontinued based on this snapshot, it would be Product C.

The problem with a data snapshot like this, however, is that it gives you no insight into how many of your customers have actually tried each of these products, or how happy they have been with them. To see these effects, rather than a snapshot you need to see a "movie" of how your customers' behaviors are changing over time. You need longitudinal insight.

So now let's suppose that, in addition to POS data, you have a loyalty program that provides the merchandising manager with longitudinal customer data, based on comparing each member's transactions from week to week and month to month. This new data would allow her to see the frequency with which members purchase each of these products. And she could see how many of her customers have tried a product at least once, as well as the number who have re-purchased. The new table, with longitudinal data based on customer-specific tracking, might look like this:

	Weekly Units	Weekly Spend	Total Stores	Spend per Store	Customer Penetration	Repeat Rate
Product A	10350	$ 26,393	267	$ 99	0.81%	4.3%
Product B	6300	$ 17,010	210	$ 81	0.55%	7.9%
Product C	5100	$ 10,965	166	$ 66	0.45%	16.0%

From this new data, providing longitudinal insight, she can clearly see that Product C is actually the company's star performer in this category, while Product A is the dog. Product C is repurchased by consumers almost four times as frequently as Product A, but revenue per store is low because less than one out of every 200 of your customers has even sampled it yet.

So rather than discontinuing Product C, your merchandising manager should consider promoting trial with some coupons or two-for-one deals (offered through the loyalty program to those customers who haven't yet bought it). After all, the more customers buy this product, the more loyalty and revenue it will generate.

If you don't have customer-specific data you can't get a realistic view of how your customers buy from you. And if your business model is one where customers have traditionally bought without providing any form of identification, then a loyalty program is a great way to acquire this kind of insight.

Five Best Practices for Loyalty Programs

The most effective kind of loyalty program is one that either uses the information provided by a customer's rewarded behavior to provide longitudinal insight and to fashion more relevant, customer-specific services or offers, or one that uses the rewards themselves to incentivize loyalty in a category in which customers' needs are not so differentiated.

As these kinds of programs have proliferated, however, and as customers themselves have become more interconnected and knowledgeable through social media, the best loyalty programs also seem to be characterized by five important best practices, which I often recommend to companies. There are lots of other considerations, but if you're thinking about a loyalty program for your business, or if you're trying to upgrade your current one, then these five best practices can serve as a quick checklist:

1. *Never waste an opportunity to gain insight about a customer.* An effective loyalty program will offer a choice of services or treatments in order to reveal more about a customer's personal preferences. Providing points in return for completing surveys or responding to inquiries can generate a wealth of insights, but so can more specific offers designed to illuminate different customers' different motivations. A financial services firm, for instance, could improve insights into a customer's needs and investment perspective by offering a mix of awards based on either lifetime accomplishment or short-term behaviors. With an appropriate mix of awards you could even encourage customers to specify their prizes in advance of earning the points needed to redeem them, in order to gain these insights earlier.

2. *An effective program offers modularity, enabling participants to mix and match aspects to their own preferences.* Modular offerings are a practical way to allow for customer-driven personalization of a program without going to the extreme of full customization. Key aspects of the program, like member qualification, can be developed with several alternatives, and customers can be offered a set of guided choices to select from. A sophisticated marketing approach would offer different sets of choices for different groups of customers based on their value—so everybody wouldn't be choosing from the same set. For example, a lower value customer might choose from rewards alternatives that include a service upgrade, while high-value customers might have choices that include additional redemptions or alternative merchandise. In addition, modularity will allow a program to incorporate partners and co-sponsors more easily, which will broaden the appeal of a program and enlist higher enrollment.

3. *Consumers value openness. So be sure your program works with other programs.* The more open your loyalty program is, the more beneficial and attractive it will be to customers. Transferable points and rewards offer the customer the greatest flexibility in using program earnings. As you gain customer insight, your program can mature into a more open proposition without endangering customer loyalty, because the barrier to a customer's switching will no longer be purely economic (i.e., the value of the points earned), but convenience (having to "teach" another program about individual desires and preferences). Openness is inevitable in loyalty marketing programs, and companies must choose whether to lead the charge, or to react to it. If your competitors' points or miles are available for purchase on the open market (as is already the case with many airline frequent flyer programs, for instance), you may even want to allow your best customers to redeem the points you issue for prizes offered by your direct competitors! Think about it: if you run an airline, wouldn't you want to know what competitor airlines your best customers also like to fly on?

4. *A loyalty program should be managed around customers, not products.* Align the organization and administration of your program around certain identified sets of customers, and then measure your marketing managers by the impact they have on the behaviors of these different groups. This is the most direct way to make progress in each customer segment, and to improve the loyalty (and lifetime values) of the individual customers in each segment.

5. *Above all else: simplicity.* The fewer rules and restrictions you have, the more engaging your program will be for the customer. It's better to narrow your offers to those you can deliver consistently, rather than including elements that can't be relied upon. Airline programs frequently suffer, for instance, when they publicize high-value redemptions that turn out not to be very readily available. Such offers often do more harm than good, by unnecessarily raising customer expectations and then not delivering. If you can't deliver consistently on whatever reward you promote within your loyalty program, you not only damage your program's credibility, but you could undermine trust in your whole brand.

CHAPTER 13

Life in the Frictionless Fast Lane

As technology continues its steady march, it is inevitable that customers will seek out more paths of least resistance. They will resent friction and avoid those companies that waste any more of their time or effort than absolutely necessary.

And customers will be more in charge. They'll have their own tools and technologies. Today's big-company customer analytics program is tomorrow's smartphone app for consumers.

The Consumer of the Future Will Be an Algorithm

Professional basketball player Jeremy Lin graduated from Harvard in 2010 with a degree in economics and a 3.1 GPA, but despite his great college basketball playing he went undrafted by the NBA that year. It was only after the New York Knicks lost two guards to injuries early in the 2011-12 season that they signed him at all. And of course, to the great surprise of the team's management, Lin went on to electrify fans, scoring an average of 27 points a game in six consecutive wins.

But what is fascinating about the "Linsanity" story is that nearly two years before Lin started his first Knicks game there was one man, Ed Weiland, who predicted Lin's success based on what his own unique algorithm said about the kid's college playing statistics. In May 2010 on his basketball stats blog[14], Weiland wrote, "If he can get the passing thing down and handle the point, Jeremy Lin is a good enough player to start in the NBA and possibly star." The amazing thing is that Weiland wasn't a professional scout, nor was he a statistician. He was just an avid basketball fan with a personal computer. He made his living driving a FedEx truck.

Many of us don't appreciate just how empowering Big Data will soon be for ordinary people. We look at data as a corporate tool – "they" are tracking "us," and we can only hope that the big corporations with all this data will use it humanely.

But Big Data can also directly benefit consumers themselves. What will happen within a few years, almost inevitably, is that business algorithms will be making the offers, while consumer algorithms will be making the buying decisions.

We can already see the outline of this model beginning to take shape. Maybe you remember Farecast, the service that predicted when a particular airfare was likely to be going up or down, prior to flight. By drawing on 175 billion previous airfare data points and applying rigorous analytics, the service claimed to be able to predict when an airfare would go up or down in the next week, with an accuracy of more than 70 percent. Founded by computer scientist and University of Washington professor Oren Etzioni, Farecast was acquired by Microsoft for $115 million in 2008.

After selling Farecast to Microsoft, however, Etzioni launched another price-forecasting service called Decide.com, which used even more data and analytics to predict future price changes on a whole range of consumer products. This company was eventually acquired by eBay.

Following in Etzioni's footsteps, personalized shopping sites like StitchFix, Trunk Club, Club W, and Birchbox use algorithms and mine data to personalize clothing, wine selections, and beauty products for direct-to-consumer markets.

My point is that your own shopping activities in the not-too-distant future will likely be sharpened with highly sophisticated data and analytics tools. And you won't have to have a computer science degree either. You'll have access to these tools even if your day job is driving a FedEx truck.

If I Ran a Brick-and-Mortar Retailer

E-commerce vendors pose a very serious threat to brick-and-mortar retailers, because today's shoppers are never more than a click away from comparing prices. As difficult as it is to compete with online vendors, however, there are still a few strategies available to smart brick-and-mortar retailers.

The first big problem for physical stores is that online operators typically face lower inventory and service costs, not to mention the overhead savings represented by not having to maintain retail outlets. So their prices are generally lower than you can find in a physical store. To compete, the first thing I would do is supplement my store's regular, physical-products-in-the-store business with online products delivered from warehouses.

Once I had a relatively robust online offering, I would actively encourage my in-store customers to supplement their physical shopping with online information, perhaps posting QR codes alongside product information, so customers with smartphones could immediately access our website to drill down into more detailed product specifications or read other customers' reviews. Right there in the store.

Or, as John Lewis is doing, I would equip my in-store salespeople with tablets providing them access to our online offerings and to the previously expressed online preferences of the customers they're dealing with right now, in the store.

Either way, I would allow a shopper to buy a product in the store and walk out with it right then, or wait a day or two and have it delivered from the warehouse, for a slightly lower price. Even doing this, however, it's unlikely I'd be able to match the lower costs of a pure online vendor. I can come closer, but I'll have a hard time closing the gap entirely (and don't forget that online vendors sometimes still have a big sales-tax advantage).

If I sold more complex products, however, such as electronics, appliances, cars, or something like building supplies, I would also offer services such as installation, maintenance, and repair, along with the products sold in my store. A car dealer with a great service reputation, for instance, is likely to generate better car sales, even when facing competition from no-service vendors selling the same cars for less. I'd want customers to feel that buying a difficult-to-install product from my store could still be a completely frictionless experience.

But I wouldn't stop there. I'd work hard to improve the customer experience within my store, in order to make the process of *shopping* into something pleasurable, interesting, or exciting itself. When Target puts a Starbucks in front of the cashiers' stations, or when a bookstore adds a reading lounge and brings in authors for book signings, they're trying to create an experience worth coming in for, or at least one that is pleasant and not to be avoided.

The kind of customer experience I would try to create, however, would be one that is as personalized and welcoming as possible. I would hire positive, friendly salespeople, and I would train them in how to remember names and faces. I would encourage all in-store employees to engage shoppers in conversations, rather than sales pitches alone. I would teach my salespeople to proactively watch out for our customers' interests at all times – providing each customer with the soundest, most objective advice and help possible, no matter whether the customer buys from us this time or not.

Trustability has the potential to change the entire framework of competition, because it can engage an individual customer's empathy. So I would want my salespeople treating the customer just the way they themselves would like to be treated if they were the customer. When we proactively watch out for our customers' interests, our customers will *want* us to succeed.

Trustability engages people's natural impulse to show empathy. As a result, when trustability is used as a competitive business strategy it actually transcends the commercial domain of monetary metrics and incentives, and taps into the social domain of friendship, sharing, and reciprocity. Rather than simply calculating the dollar value of product features and pricing, an empathetic customer is more likely to take into account the "feelings" of the business itself, because the customer experience is now based not just on buying and selling, but on *humanity*.

And that's the biggest single advantage my brick-and-mortar store could have over any competitive vendor, online or off.

If all of this sounds too airy-fairy to you, then I suggest you take a look at a few retailers who have used these strategies quite successfully already. In Connecticut, Zane's Cycles, founded by Chris Zane, is a good example. Or look at the family of clothing stores owned and operated by the Mitchell family. Or check out the Sewell Automotive family of car dealerships in Dallas.

Carl Sewell, Chris Zane, and Jack Mitchell have all written books based on these and other, similar ideas that made their own brick-and-mortar retailing businesses successful, in spite of the onslaught of online competition.

The Twilight of the Corporate Call Center

In November 2014, The Coca Cola Company announced to its employees that it was doing away with voicemail[15] at its corporate headquarters in Atlanta.

Who does voicemail any more, anyway? It's always been a hassle. The demise of voicemail has been predicted[16] for years. Still, there is a bigger issue here, involving the fact that voice communication, for all its advantages, also has some serious disadvantages:

- The voice channel is *slow*. Think about it. When we're reading a text message, whether email or SMS or something else, we can scan it at our own speed, skipping over the fluff and re-reading or carefully thinking about the important information.

- The voice channel can't be multiplexed. We can have several email or text-messaging conversations going on at once, but we can't really pay attention to more than one voice conversation at a time.

- An audible voice generates the most unstructured of unstructured data. Before it can be transformed into other data (such as text) it has to be analyzed and re-analyzed, and a computer can only parse the real meaning of a voice message *after* it has first been rendered into text.

OK, so now think about the primary purpose of most corporate call centers. Start with the fact that more than half of the phone calls made to U.S. call centers today are preceded by an online session of some kind – a customer trying to find the answer to a question, or scheduling a service visit, or buying something. For most of us, it's only when we can't solve our problem online that we resort to a call in the first place. Having to make a call rather than being able to work things out directly on a company's website or within its mobile app is a hassle. It's friction. The voice channel is slow and cumbersome.

For almost any kind of routine transaction, most people would *prefer* to deal with a machine rather than a person, because automated processes are totally frictionless. Ever since the advent of ATMs, for instance, you can count on the fingers of one hand the number of people who prefer to go into a physical bank branch and interact with a teller, just to get cash or deposit a check.

At today's call centers, the vast majority of reps sit in front of their computer screens (often multiple screens), and as inquiries, reservations, or service requests come in, they access their company's computer systems with their keyboards. They dig for answers or solutions, and then they relay what their computers have said back to the customers.

Today's call center associate, in other words, is simply "human middleware." He or she is the manual, human interface between a company's computers and its customers.

Increasingly, these human interactions and conversations are taking place in non-voice channels. Online chats and email exchanges with customers are already common enough that many call centers are actually more properly referred to as "contact" centers. Moreover, cloud computing now permits more customer interactions to be handled by at-home agents, or even by a company's in-store retail staff when they are available, so the word "center" is no longer really accurate.

Today's computers are getting better at recognizing voice inputs, especially for simple things ("Please say or enter your account number..."), while the computer systems feeding the call center associates' screens are also improving rapidly, as they become simpler and more intuitive to access. So we could easily conclude that the corporate call center will soon go the way of voicemail, or the teller window, but this is where the analogy breaks down.

Because there is one thing an actual human voice provides to a customer that a computer will never be able to provide: *humanity*. Customers are people, and people want empathy and caring from other people, especially if they are frustrated, or anxious, or unhappy. They want a human being to hear them out, to commiserate, and to provide emotional support.

We may not want to waste time by going to the teller window for a simple cash transaction, but most of us wouldn't dream of undertaking a new mortgage without meeting a loan officer face to face.

Yes, routine tasks are rapidly being automated away, but that leaves the really tough jobs – the kinds of problems that can't be solved with a line of code.

So watch for corporate call centers to be replaced by *humanity* centers over the next few years. Rather than simply accessing and relaying computerized instructions, tomorrow's associates will be tasked with listening to customers, absorbing their feedback, and providing empathetic support and advice, as a way to ensure their continued loyalty.

The primary mission of tomorrow's contact center will be delivering humanity to customers, and that is a mission very well-suited to voice interaction.

Turn Customer Frustration Into Opportunity

Fully automated, bot-provided customer care will be available to all, sooner or later. But for now, good customer service remains a people-intensive task simply because human customers continue to need other human beings to understand, analyze, and solve many of the kinds of problems that come up on the products and services they use.

The problem is that many businesses continue to treat customer service as simply a cost of doing business, rather than as an opportunity to connect with their customers. As customers, we all know the frustration of trying to reach a real human being when we call that toll-free number. And the more difficult a company makes it to reach a live rep on the phone, the angrier we get.

One recent survey[17] by Arizona State University shows that consumer frustration and "rage" at cost-constrained, robotically provided customer care has soared in recent years, as companies have continued to automate solely to reduce their costs. According to the survey, overall customer satisfaction with customer service was no higher than in 1976, nearly 40 years ago. Consumers are "frustrated that there are too many automated response menus, there aren't enough customer care agents, they waste a lot of time dealing with the problem, and they have to contact the company an average of four times to get resolution."

There's even a website, GetHuman.com, dedicated to compiling the quickest ways, at different companies' call centers, to exit the answer robot and get to a live human being. To reach DIRECTV in the U.S., for example, dial 800-531-5000, and "press 0# each time it asks for your number, then say 'Customer Service,' then press 6." Or for British Telecom in the U.K., dial 0800-800150 and then "press * 0 each time you hear an automated voice."

A business that thinks solely about the *cost* of handling customer calls, however, rather than the *opportunities* they represent, is operating in a short-sighted and ultimately self-destructive manner. If your company has ever considered how to create better engagement with customers, then making direct voice contact with a customer at a time when he or she is often frustrated and under stress should be seen as a great opportunity.

Putting an authentic human being on the other end of an inbound phone call is the most cost-efficient mechanism for showing genuine *empathy* with a customer when things do go wrong, as they inevitably will, at least occasionally. One of the principle roles for your company's call center, in other words, is to show a human face to your customers economically, and at scale.

Smart, forward-thinking companies know this. Capital One 360, for instance, is Capital One's online bank (formerly ING Direct), and it prides itself on answering every call with a real person. But one of the tricks to this is that the online tools are truly efficient and can easily handle virtually every routine inquiry or transaction, without flaw.

And one of the more interesting recent developments in call centers is the increasing use of at-home or remote reps for handling calls. Your contact center associates no longer really need to sit within any particular "center" at all. New technologies allow a business to route its customer service calls directly and seamlessly to a rep's own location, while using cloud-based software to safely and securely manage the rep's computer during the interaction process. Obviously, this diminishes the need for a building, with all its desks and cubicles, along with the need for the reps themselves to drive their cars into work, park in the lot, and so forth.

As a result, an increasing number of customer care calls today are in fact being handled from remote locations – mothers with kids at school, professionals with particular expertise or skills, and even retail service people who make themselves available during slow times at store locations.

Besides the sheer convenience factor, cloud technology now makes it possible for any business with a peak season to staff up and down almost instantly. A retailer with a heavy Christmas shopping season, or a tax-preparation service with a heavy March and April load, or a healthcare firm during the enrollment season can quickly add pre-qualified at-home reps to its remote sales and customer care staff without having to plan and take ownership of new facilities months ahead of time. Nor does staffing up for peak season require months or years of systems work, integration, and new IT facilities, either.

Over time, automated interactions, web and mobile apps, and other self-service tools will inevitably displace a larger and larger proportion of customer care functions.

But this just makes the *human* opportunity even more important. Because as more customers take advantage of these online tools, a higher proportion of actual *calls* are likely to be the result of failed self-service experiences, so the vast majority of these callers will already be frustrated.

More and more, simply answering the phone will present a great opportunity to improve your reputation as a business. A customer who begins his or her journey in frustration, but who then encounters an empathetic voice, will have experienced your company's "human face," and that will likely be the best customer experience of all.

At-Home Reps Can Improve Your Health

In addition to workforce flexibility, at-home company associates give a company the ability to provide customers with a number of more complex professional services – services that would be hard to provide through staffing up contact "centers," because of the nature of the professionals involved.

In the healthcare category, for instance, at-home agents are playing an increasingly important role. One of the biggest supply constraints in this category is the availability of a doctor's time. We all have had the experience of traveling to the doctor's office, signing in, waiting for a half hour or more, having a nurse weigh us and take our blood pressure, and then… Voila! The doctor appears, and within 5 or 10 minutes he or she confirms the numbers, chats with us a bit about the problem, prescribes a drug or an x-ray or some other treatment, and then moves on to the next patient, who has now been weighed and prepped. It's an assembly line based on optimizing the use of the doctor's time, which is the scarcest resource in the value chain.

But what about patients with chronic conditions who need more constant attention? In the U.S., the Affordable Care Act (ACA) has now made healthcare outreach services reimbursable, which means that a provider or payer can follow up with patients, perhaps to confirm that they've taken their medicines, or maybe just to find out how they're feeling. This is a more critical function than you might think, because a large percentage of patients don't follow through with taking their medicine.

Athena Health, a new and innovative public company in the business of processing medical insurance claims, has found that an astounding 50 percent of all doctors' orders are not acted on. Just think about that fact for a minute. What it means is that about half the time, a doctor's prescription isn't filled by the patient, or treatments are simply not carried out. Athena knows this because one of its lines of business involves matching up the diagnoses and prescriptions ordered by physicians with the individual insurance claims filed by the patients.

In the healthcare business they call this a "compliance" problem, and it is significant.

Personal phone calls, made by trained nurses, are almost guaranteed to increase the compliance rate, greatly improving healthcare outcomes. So this kind of medical outreach program represents a big opportunity for improving care.

The problem is, since everything is already operating at nearly full capacity, how can healthcare professionals afford to take even more time for this new task? One solution is to employ at-home nurses to make these outreach calls. Some may be retired, while others may have their own children to care for, and others simply prefer not to have to commute in to a hospital or medical facility.

Moreover, because different kinds of patients and diseases require different kinds of treatments, using at-home medical professionals to perform this outreach function allows a healthcare plan to do a better job of matching the skills and experience levels of different professionals to the needs of different patients. An at-home nurse in Boise, Idaho could talk or chat with a diabetes patient in Ocala, Florida.

By matching the widely dispersed talent available in the healthcare category to the widely dispersed needs of our population, everyone can in fact get more personalized – and effective – care.

CHAPTER 14

Caution: Good Intentions Required

We began this book with technology, and technology hasn't stopped improving. Disruptive innovations will likely continue to be one of the most significant characteristics of the business landscape for the foreseeable future.

But how can you survive the next disruptive innovation in your own business category? Will your customers stick with you? Will they even *care* whether you succeed?

No matter what business model you launch, or which strategy you pursue, or what technology you master, the only way to survive this period of rapid and dramatic technological change is to have your customers' goodwill and support. And nothing will garner that support faster than your good intentions.

Knowledgeable Customers Create More Value

A few years ago three professors did an interesting study on the amount of value created by different customers from their own spending, as compared to their referrals of other customers. They looked at one financial services firm and one telco, modeling each firm's customers to try to assess the amount of lifetime value produced by direct spending, as well as by referring other customers who spent. They wrote their study up in a *Harvard Business Review* article, "How Valuable is Word of Mouth?[18]" which is highly readable and has a number of very interesting points.

Somewhat counterintuitively, one thing they discovered was that the highest spending customers are not the same as those who generate the most value by referring others (at least not according to their model). To help visualize this, I took the numbers from the telco company they analyzed, and I arranged them on a bar chart:

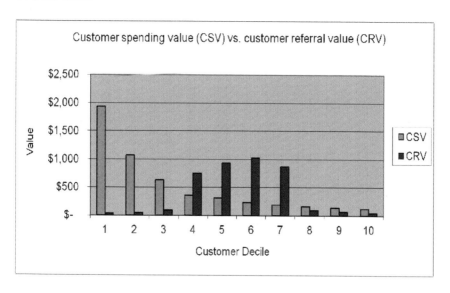

This chart clearly shows that the top three spending (CSV) deciles don't overlap at all with the top three referral (CRV) deciles. Or in plain English, the 30 percent of customers who spend the most are completely different from the

30 percent who refer the most other customers. Not even close. Big spenders generate little value at all with their referrals of other customers, while those who generate the most value from referring others tend to be middling spenders themselves.

The authors of this study didn't speculate as to why this seemed to be true of both the telco and the financial services firm, but if you think about it, it easily makes sense. You may spend more yourself on a product or service because you have a greater need for it, so that makes you a high-CSV customer.

But the customers who refer the most other customers are more likely to do so not because of their personal spending levels, but because they are the kinds of people whose opinions their friends and colleagues value. They have "authority" with their friends. They are known for their expertise and credibility.

This dichotomy, between high spending and high reference value, becomes more important every day, as technology continues to connect us more seamlessly with our friends and colleagues. Personal expertise has never been more easily shared with others, nor has it ever been easier to evaluate and rate other customers' authority and expertise – even when you don't know them personally.

For businesses, this means it's more important than ever to cultivate relationships not just with the highest spending customers, but with the most knowledgeable ones as well. Too many businesses still regard *less* knowledgeable customers as high-value targets. But in the e-social era, the less knowledgeable the customer is, the less likely it is that he or she will ever generate much actual "word of mouth" value for your brand.

One more important point: In order to appeal to knowledgeable customers, you have to do more than provide a discount or even a unique product benefit. You need to earn their trust, as well.

Influencing the Influencers

You can buy your advertising, but you can't buy your friends.

If you want to influence the influencers in your category – if you want to generate more positive word of mouth and customer referrals from the most knowledgeable and authoritative customers – you won't be able to do so with discounts, or free gifts, or anything of monetary value. If anything, offering something like that might actually offend the customer.

Instead, you have to concentrate on earning your influencers' trust by understanding the *non-commercial* things they value.

Think of what might motivate an influential blogger or Twitter user – someone whose opinions matter to thousands of followers. While almost all such key influencers would be offended if you offered to compensate them for a favorable post, they are still human beings, and like all the rest of us they still have ambitions. They want to be noticed, and to increase their own influence, which means writing better, more original and authoritative posts.

Most such influencers don't think of themselves as experts on particular companies or brands, per se, but as authorities with respect to an issue or problem of concern to them and their followers. It might be a business issue or a health issue or a relationship issue, but in most cases their central mission isn't to evaluate the products and services offered by you or your competitors, but to help their followers and friends solve problems. Expressing their opinions about brands and products is more likely to be a side effect of this mission.

Think about social media influence in this context and you'll realize that what social media mavens value most are the signals and ingredients of influence itself: acknowledgment, recognition, information, and access. You can remember them easily with the mnemonic word "aria," as in the solo sung by your favorite opera star.

Acknowledgment: Simply identifying an influential blogger or social media influencer and acknowledging their existence will go a long way toward having a positive influence. So when you identify someone important, reach out by posting a comment on their blog, retweeting a smart update, or emailing them with a thoughtful (but non-self-serving) suggestion. Just let them know you're paying attention.

Recognition: Consider mentioning authoritative bloggers in your own press communications, providing recognition to the blogger as well as additional sources for whatever reporters or other commentators follow your firm. And, if you have a crowd service system that relies on a few super-users to handle the complicated inquiries of other customers, then recognize them with special badges, emblems, or status designations. Everyone wants to be Platinum in something.

Information: Key influencers want the inside dope, the straight skinny, so provide them with all the information you can reasonably manage. Even without divulging the kind of "inside" information that might get a public company in trouble, you can almost certainly provide a key influencer with a more useful perspective and insight about your business or your category, including the problems you face, threats you are trying to avoid, and opportunities you see.

Access: Just as useful as insightful information is giving an influencer access to the author of the insight, or the operating person at your business who is most connected to the information. Probably nothing will pay bigger dividends in terms of social media influence than simply allowing influencers themselves to have access to some of your own people, experts, and authorities. Not everyone gets this kind of access, because you just can't take the time for everyone. But do take the time for someone who has an important enough following in social media.

There's a caveat to this, of course: No matter how influential you may become with your own social media influencers, in the end it will always be their call.

So your ultimate goal with social media influencers is to establish a level of mutual trust that will serve as a bridge, increasing your credibility with them by increasing their own credibility with their followers. And then it's up to them, not you.

The Smothering Downside of Personalization

Increasingly, we are surrounded by personalization – retail stores offering special deals based on your shopping history, websites serving up news based on what you've clicked on in the past, and marketers selecting the right message for you based on where you live, what else you own, and what you've actually bought (or not bought) before.

As one of the very first proponents of personalized marketing, I should be extremely pleased with myself. Just the other day, a news editor emailed me to say "Countless people have said to me in the past month alone, 'Now is the time for true one-to-one marketing [and at scale]. Now we have the technology to make this a reality.'"

There are many benefits to personalization. You can get individually customized products, from blue jeans or running shoes to bicycles or cars. You can order custom-printed M&Ms and custom-labeled bottled water. Movie and book recommendations come tailored to your interests. And because companies remember your data and preferences, you don't have to tell an online store where you live or what your credit card details are, nor do you need 10 minutes to complete a new form or contract every time you book a hotel room or rent a car.

But customization has a downside, too. From the very beginning, whenever I talked about the benefits of personalization, one or two people would take me aside to point out some of this downside. For instance, the more you get your news online, the more likely it is that the websites you get your news from will adapt to your interests. Click on a story about your college basketball team, and news about that team will be more likely to be displayed to you the next time you log in. But this means that stories about homelessness, or genocide in Africa, or the latest technology innovation, are less likely to be displayed. They'll still be there, they'll just be one more level down, one more click away from your attention span.

We used to call this the "serendipity" argument for un-personalizing your news. When you leaf through a printed newspaper, printed up the same way for everyone, you are more likely to encounter news or information by sheer luck or happenstance. The industrial espionage story just happens to lie next to the story about your company's product launch, or the story about battered women is on the same page as the one about a new fitness technique you're interested in.

The problem is, when you surf the news online, there's very little serendipity. Instead, personalized information will tend to smother you with sameness and familiarity, reducing the opportunity for learning new things, or seeing things from a different perspective. An algorithm has clocked your past views and clicks, and quantitatively gauged the placement of today's articles in terms of their likelihood to interest you.

This is just one aspect of the argument explored in Ira Pariser's 2011 book *The Filter Bubble: How the New Personalized Web is Changing What We Read and How We Think*. It's not a new argument, but it's more important today than it was just a few years ago.

Today, *everything* seems to be personalized. Advertising messages and product pitches are designed to show you things you are more likely to buy, and (not surprisingly) what you bought yesterday is highly relevant to what you might buy today. According to statistics Pariser cites, more than a third of Americans under 30 already get their news primarily from social networking sites.

One of the problems with personalization is that it runs on algorithms, and these algorithms (at present, anyway) are locked in to presenting new things based on history or data already collected. This means, rather than discovering new facts or perspectives when you search for news, information, or products, you will be presented with "adjacent" concepts. It's not so much discovery of new ideas as it is exploitation of existing ideas.

According to Pariser, if you talk to a tech person involved in crafting personalization strategies, you'll learn that one of the biggest obstacles to progress is we could call the "local maximum" problem. Presenting someone with better ideas or news about any particular product or concept will inevitably lead toward the best possible news or information *about that particular item*. But it will also exclude other, unrelated news or information that might in fact be highly relevant to the user. And this kind of filtering can easily cascade on you based on relatively inconsequential actions. As Pariser says, "clicking on a link about gardening or anarchy or Ozzy Osbourne" will in turn supply you with "more information on the topic, which you're more inclined to click on because the topic has now been primed for you."

A "filter bubble" like this, moreover, depresses your curiosity, because it is designed to speak to your known and already-expressed information desires. You are less likely to encounter the serendipitous article on gene splicing or The World Cup or the typhoon in The Philippines – articles that *might* have triggered your interest had you just been exposed to them.

As a result of all this personalization technology, Pariser maintains that consumers are more exploited for our known preferences and desires, while citizens are becoming more narrow-minded and insular in their thinking. People have always preferred associating with others who share the same philosophical or political views, and now we hardly even need to be exposed to people who disagree with us.

This would be a dangerous situation for any democratic society, and we should pay attention.

How to Avoid Being Smothered by a Personalized World

A Frenchman walks into a bar with a duck on his head, and the bartender asks, "Hey, where'd you get that?" So the duck says "I got it in Paris, they've got millions of 'em there."

This joke is funny because the punch line just doesn't fit with the "context" of the setup. It violates our expectations, and this gives it the power to give us a chuckle.

Human beings are constantly observing the environment in order to make mental predictions for what will happen next, given the context of their observations. I've already written about how important context is when it comes to delivering a truly frictionless customer experience. The deeper the context of a relationship—that is, the more detailed or informative your previous interactions with a customer have been—the more loyal that customer is likely to be in the future, because (among other things) the customer just doesn't want to have to re-teach one of your competitors what he or she has already spent time and effort teaching you.

But context is also a key to innovation and creativity, which are context-dependent, and to overcoming the smothering effect of increased personalization. In this case, however, rather than using context to make predictions about our environment, creative ideas come when we purposely *violate* context. Context violations produce things you don't expect, from funny punch lines to innovative ideas.

Your most creative insights are almost always the result of taking an idea that works in one domain and applying it in a different context. Every "new" idea you have, personally, is based on some combination of previous concepts in your own mind, even if you combined these concepts subconsciously. In a sense, as Matt Ridley has observed[19], innovation occurs when ideas get together and "have sex" with each other. In evolutionary terms, it's called "exaptation." Bird feathers, for instance, are thought to have evolved during the Cretaceous period to help land-based reptiles protect themselves from the cold, but when one species of reptile later began experimenting with gliding, feathers were exapted as excellent tools for controlling air flow.

Innovation thrives on context violations and exaptation. The anti-lock braking system in your car is a result of research and development originally done in the field of aviation, for example. Icy airplane runways can't be sprayed with salt and gravel to assist in slowing a speeding plane, so anti-lock brakes were first invented in this domain. Computer punch cards were exapted from the punch cards originally conceived to drive weaving patterns on mechanized looms. Viagra was originally developed as a drug to reduce hypertension.

The problem with an increasingly personalized world is that context is harder and harder to violate. You have to work at it more.

And it's uncomfortable. As human beings we're all biased to prefer the routine and familiar, as opposed to the new and different. We feel safer when we know what's going to happen next and we're more comfortable talking to people whose views we share.

But humanity is not just about empathy. It's also about creativity. Putting humanity into your company's customer experience requires both. So here are a few ideas to stimulate your own creativity, by intentionally breaking the context of your current thoughts and beliefs:

- Read a magazine you would never ordinarily have the least interest in.

- Pick a point of view you vehemently disagree with, and argue in favor of it instead. Be convincing.

- At a restaurant, order a food you normally can't stand, and eat it.

- Put your clothes on in a different order every day (i.e., shirt first one day, socks first the next, right then left instead of left then right, and so forth).

- At a party, find the person you have least in common with and spend at least an hour in conversation with them.

- Drive a different route to work or school, or to church, or to the club. Take a long cut, on purpose.

- Memorize something useless but ambitious, like pi to 100 digits, or the names of all the major chess openings, or all the U.S. vice presidents and the presidents they served.

- Meet one new person a day for a whole month, either in person or online. Converse with them, get to know them.

The Competitive Advantage of Trustability

Not long ago I had to fly from Jacksonville to New York on JetBlue. The flight experienced some mechanical problems before takeoff and ended up almost six hours late. Everyone was terribly inconvenienced.

But when we exited the plane at JFK, each passenger was given a letter from JetBlue apologizing for the delay, and notifying us that because of the incident we were each entitled to compensation under JetBlue's Customer Bill of Rights[20].

Here's what stood out about JetBlue's action: Rather than asking me to log in to its website and fill in my flight information and confirmation number, or to mail in my boarding pass or something, the airline said passengers didn't need to do anything at all to claim their refunds, just wait a couple of days and the appropriate credit would automatically be posted to their "Flight Bank" at JetBlue, to be immediately available for use on future bookings!

Because most of JetBlue's competitors make you jump through a few hoops before getting a refund, they enjoy a "breakage" on refund claims of 10 percent or more. That is, 10 percent or more of the customers who are entitled to refunds from an airline simply fail to claim them, so these airlines get to keep that money.

And not long ago, Amazon began paying refunds to customers even before they ask! As reported by Bloomberg[21], Amazon "has built automated systems that detect when a customer hasn't paid the lowest available price for a product, or when the playback of a streaming movie is shoddy, and doles out refunds."

Amazon and JetBlue are like poster children for trustability.

But what would prompt these two otherwise intelligent companies voluntarily to give up the "free money" that comes from making customers go through a process to claim their refunds? Why would any company protect its customers' financial interests proactively, even when its competitors do not, and it costs real money to do so?

Well, in his 2013 letter[22] to Amazon's shareholders, CEO Jeff Bezos explained that his company's customer-centric focus has many advantages in terms of innovation, agility, competition, and investment priorities. And it is because of Amazon's intense focus on the customer that it implements such proactively trustworthy policies. According to Bezos:

> "One advantage – perhaps a somewhat subtle one – of a customer-driven focus is that it aids a certain type of proactivity. When we're at our best, we don't wait for external pressures. We are internally driven to improve our services, adding benefits and features, before we have to. We lower prices and increase value for customers before we have to. We invent before we have to. These investments are motivated by customer focus rather than by reaction to competition. We think this approach earns more trust with customers and drives rapid improvements in customer experience – importantly – even in those areas where we are already the leader."

If you're not focused on your customer's experience – if understanding what's in the customer's interest and being proactive about protecting that interest is not your absolute top priority as a business – then you're probably not going to be as agile, innovative, and competitive. It's that simple.

So go ahead, bank those profits from unclaimed customer refunds and other mistakes and oversights on your customers' part. Have a ball, in the short term. But realize that in the long term you won't be around.

You'll have been replaced by some other competitor – perhaps a start-up – that delivers a genuinely human, empathetic, and frictionless customer experience.

Transformational Leadership for the E-Social World

It used to be simpler for business leaders, when workers all gathered in the same physical building or place of business, and authority could be diagrammed into neat organizational charts. It used to be that you could build and operate a large company mostly by applying "transactional leadership" – that is, by using rewards and penalties to ensure that each worker's self-interest was aligned with the company's top-down instructions and goals.

But that was then, and this is now. Today's companies deal primarily with information-intensive tasks, and decisions must be made by networked groups of employees and partners working collaboratively, connected by technology. Not only that, but an ever larger proportion of employees work from home or on the road, from sales executives and research analysts to rank-and-file customer service reps.

These kinds of organizations call for a more nuanced style of leadership – transformational leadership – which engages employees by appealing to more intrinsic motivations such as autonomy, fulfillment, mastery, a sense of purpose, and a spirit of camaraderie at work. Engaged employees will bind together to achieve the common goal. And, social cohesiveness like this is what can motivate an individual to forego his or her own self-interest when it's necessary to further the group's mission.

So the problem today's leaders face is how to promote social cohesiveness in an increasingly dispersed and independently functioning organization.

In his excellent book on moral philosophy *The Righteous Mind*, Jonathan Haidt argues that social binding is one of the secrets of the human race's extraordinary rise, and that some cultural attributes of human society, such as religion or patriotism, actually inspire people to be willing to sacrifice their very lives for the benefit of the larger group. Military exercises such as marching in step work well for armies precisely because they trigger our "hiving" instinct – our desire to find fulfillment as a part of a bigger group.

Buried within Haidt's book were some interesting and somewhat counterintuitive suggestions for how business leaders might do a better job of triggering this group-protection instinct and generating "hivishness" within their own organizations. If you want your employees to be "self organizing," even though they may report up through different lines, as well as being geographically dispersed, you might find this advice helpful.

In Haidt's words (p. 276 of his book):

> *The hive switch may be more of a slider switch than an on-off switch, and with a few institutional changes you can create environments that will nudge everyone's sliders a bit closer to the hive position. For* example:
>
> - *Increase similarity, not diversity. To make a human hive, you want to make everyone feel like a family. So don't call attention to racial and ethnic differences; make them less relevant by ramping up similarity and celebrating the group's shared values and common identity. A great deal of research in social psychology shows that people are warmer and more trusting toward people who look like them, dress like them, talk like them, or even just share their first name or birthday. There's nothing special about race. You can make people care less about race by drowning race differences in a sea of similarities, shared goals, and mutual interdependencies.*
>
> - *Exploit synchrony. People who move together are saying, "We are one, we are a team..." Japanese corporations such as Toyota begin their days with synchronous companywide exercises. Groups prepare for battle— in war and sports—with group chants and ritualized movements... If it's too creepy to ask your employees or fellow group members to do synchronized calisthenics, perhaps you can just try to have more parties with dancing or karaoke. Synchrony builds trust.*
>
> - *Create healthy competition among teams, not individuals.... [S]oldiers don't risk their lives for their country or for the army; they do so for their buddies in the same squad or platoon. Studies show that intergroup competition increases love of the in-group far more than it increases dislike of the out-group. Intergroup competitions, such as friendly rivalries*

between corporate divisions, or intramural sports competitions, should have a net positive effect on hivishness and social capital. But pitting individuals against each other in a competition for scarce resources (such as bonuses) will destroy hivishness, trust, and morale.

If you're a leader in a modern, information-intensive organization, it makes sense to focus a bit of your time on boosting the level of camaraderie – the spirit of shared purpose and social cohesion – in your organization. In the long term, it may be the single most important factor in how your company adapts to threats and exploits new opportunities.

Technology's Lesson: Be Apple, Not AOL

We began this book by arguing that technology has made it possible for companies to focus attention on their customer experience, and because technology now makes it possible to do, competitive pressure demands that they do it. So the customer experience "movement" is rooted in technology.

As technological progress continues to accelerate, however, every business sooner or later becomes vulnerable to disruptive change. New business models now appear (and disappear) at Instagram speed, and any company that can't adapt itself quickly just won't survive for long.

So let's consider Apple and AOL (formerly America Online), two technology-oriented companies both launched in the early days of the Information Age. These two companies have had very different fates, however, over the last 25 years of highly disruptive technology innovation.

At the height of its power in 2001, AOL bought media giant Time Warner, enjoyed a market cap of $222 billion, and had over 30 million paying subscribers. But since then it has been a business in decline. While it earned a bit of money from operating a few interesting online properties, such as MapQuest, Huffington Post, and Moviefone, it separated from Time Warner (which remains reasonably healthy), and in 2015, after losing all but 2.2 million paying subscribers, AOL was acquired by Verizon, for $4.4 billion[23], about 2 percent of its one-time value.

Apple, by contrast, is one of the world's most valuable companies today, with a market cap over $700 billion.[24] And during the last 25 years, Apple has re-invented itself several times, moving from the PC business to the music business, to mobile phones, then tablets, and now wearables. AOL, on the other hand, somehow never managed to make the relatively simple transition from dial-up to broadband.

Of course, Apple is a perennially creative technology company, with a litany of breakthrough products. But AOL has also been highly creative, and remains committed to launching new business initiatives.

No, I think the difference between Apple and AOL that best explains the stark contrast between Apple's meteoric success and AOL's anemic survival is this:

Apple has the trust of its customers, and AOL does not.

Consider: From the very beginning, Apple based its entire business on delivering an exceptional, entirely frictionless customer experience. The company literally obsesses over the user interface of each of its products. Moreover, Apple has always tried to act in its customers' interests, because that's how it can deliver the best customer experience even if sometimes it runs against the company's own financial self-interest.

As just one example, when Apple reported weaker-than-expected earnings in April 2006, the analyst at American Technology Research attributed it to the fact that "Apple's sales representatives have been instructed to not push PowerPC Macs [on] customers who want to wait for Intel versions," presumably because the non-Intel PowerPC Mac wasn't completely up to par. The analyst went on to say that "[i]n this day and age where making numbers is important, we believe Apple is in a rare group of companies willing to sacrifice its near-term revenue opportunity for greater longer-term success by developing customer trust."

Now contrast this with AOL, a company that rapidly expanded in the early days of the Internet, but continually tried to maximize its financial results by deliberately and enthusiastically taking advantage of customer mistakes and oversights. If AOL had had a company slogan it would have been "Caveat Emptor" – or "let the buyer beware." It developed a reputation for making it ridiculously difficult to unsubscribe, and it was constantly fooling customers into paying higher fees than they needed to pay. In fact, as recently as 2011 a departing AOL senior executive told a reporter: "The dirty little secret is that 75 percent of the people who subscribe to AOL's dial-up service don't need it."

Because it has always been so focused on the customer experience, Apple's customers *want* the company to succeed. They view Apple's success as something that is clearly in their own interest. They are on Apple's side.

AOL's customers, on the other hand, are not emotionally attached to the firm's success at all. If AOL went out of business tomorrow, the company's executives might mourn its demise, but customers? Meh.

If Apple went out of business there could be rioting in every Western country.

The lesson here is that if you want your own company to survive the next inevitable technology tsunami, then focus your efforts maniacally on delivering a customer experience that is as frictionless as it can be – reliable, valuable, relevant, and trustable. Don't focus just on your short-term financials, or your current business model. Focus on your customer.

The lesson is: Be Apple, not AOL.

ENDNOTES

1 "How to Be There When Customers Ask." March 25, 2013. https://www.linkedin.com/pulse/20130315202314-17102372-how-to-be-there-when-customers-ask?trk=mp-author-card

2 "Why Facebook's New Graph Search Is No Google." http://www.fastcompany.com/3004819/why-facebooks-new-graph-search-no-google

3 "John Lewis to step up store-based omnichannel projects." http://www.retail-week.com/sectors/department-stores/john-lewis-to-step-up-store-based-omni-channel-projects/5066429.article

4 "Why Rebecca Minkoff And eBay Are Betting On Smart Dressing Rooms."http://www.fastcompany.com/3035229/the-smart-dressing-room-experiment-how-irl-shopping-is-getting-less-private-but-more-persona

5 "It's Time to Redefine Integrated Marketing." By Brian Bennett. April 16, 2013. http://www.stirstuff.com/time-to-redefine-integrated-marketing/

6 Milkin' It: A Starbucks Story. By Anna Papachristos. December 11, 2013. http://www.1to1media.com/weblog/2013/12/milkin_it_a_starbucks_story.html

7 Shopper Alert: Price May Drop for You Alone." By Stephanie Clifford. August 9, 2012. http://www.nytimes.com/2012/08/10/business/supermarkets-try-customiz-ing-prices-for-shoppers.html

8 "How Too Many Choices Can Hurt Direct Mail Response." By Hugh Chewning. February 3, 2012. http://www.articlesbase.com/marketing-tips-articles/how-too-many-choices-can-hurt-direct-mail-response-5630192.html

9 "Move Over Management! Employees Will Learn Trustability Lesson." By Don Peppers. June 24, 2010. http://www.peppersandrogersgroup.com/blog/2010/06/move-over-management-employees.html

10 "Yes, Banks Are Reordering Your Transactions And Charging Overdraft Fees." By Halah Touryalai. June 11, 2013. http://www.forbes.com/sites/

halahtouryalai/2013/06/11/yes-banks-are-reordering-your-transactions-and-charging-overdraft-fees/

11 "Why I'm Watching Deep Linking in Mobile." By John Batelle. August 18, 2014. http://battellemedia.com/archives/2014/08/need-search-economy-mobile-discovery.php

12 "CRM failure rates: 2001-2009." By Michael Krigsman. August 3, 2009. http://www.zdnet.com/article/crm-failure-rates-2001-2009/

13 "Management Decisions in a Data-Rich Environment. By Don Peppers. October 15, 2013. https://www.linkedin.com/pulse/20131015112316-17102372-management-decisions-in-a-data-rich-environment?trk=mp-reader-card

14 The story of Ed Weiland and Jeremy Lin is told in Christopher Steiner's excellent book *Automate This: How Algorithms Came to Dominate Our World* (2012)

15 "Coca Cola Disconnects Voice Mail at Headquarters." By Duane Stanford. December 22, 2014. http://www.bloomberg.com/news/articles/2014-12-22/coca-cola-disconnects-voice-mail-at-headquarters

16 "You've Got Voicemail. But Do You Care?" By Jill Colvin. April 1, 2009. http://www.nytimes.com/2009/04/02/fashion/02voicemail.html

17 "New Customer-Rage Study Out for Holiday Shopping Season." By Debbie Freeman. November 26, 2013. https://wpcarey.asu.edu/news-releases/2013-11-26/new-customer-rage-study-out-holiday-shopping-season

18 "How Valuable Is Your Word of Mouth?" By V. Kumar, J. Andrew Petersen, and Robert P. Leone. October 2007.

https://hbr.org/2007/10/how-valuable-is-word-of-mouth/ar/1

19 "When Ideas Have Sex." By Matt Ridley. July 15, 2010. http://www.huffington-post.com/tedtalks/matt-ridley-when-ideas-ha_b_647326.html

20 JetBlue's Customer Bill of Rights. http://www.jetblue.com/flying-on-jetblue/customer-protection/

21 "Amazon's Bezos Paying Refunds for Shoddy Streaming, Poor Service." By Danielle Kucera. April 12, 2013. http://www.bloomberg.com/news/articles/2013-04-12/amazon-s-bezos-paying-refunds-for-shoddy-streaming-poor-service

22 Jeff Bezos' 2013 letter to shareholders. http://www.sec.gov/Archives/edgar/data/1018724/000119312513151836/d511111dex991.htm

23 "The real reason Verizon bought AOL." By Kevin Fitchard. June 24, 2015. https://fortune.com/2015/06/24/verizon-gains-aol/

24 Forbes World's Most Valuable Brands List, 2015. http://www.forbes.com/companies/apple/